$\mathcal{S}$TRANGERS *to* THE CITY

STRANGERS *to* THE CITY

Refllections on the Beliefs and Values
of the Rule of Saint Benedict

MICHAEL CASEY
Monk of Tarrawarra

PARACLETE PRESS
BREWSTER, MASSACHUSETTS

2013 First Printing This Edition

Strangers to the City: Reflections on the Beliefs and Values of the Rule of Saint Benedict

Copyright © 2013, 2005 by Michael Casey

ISBN: 978-1-61261-397-0

The Scripture translations were made directly from the Greek or Hebrew by the author.

The translations of *The Rule of St. Benedict* were also made directly from the Latin by the author.

The original edition of *Strangers to the City* was cataloged by the Library of Congress as follows:

Library of Congress Cataloging-in-Publication Data
Casey, Michael, 1942–
Strangers to the city : reflections on the beliefs and values of the Rule of Saint Benedict / Michael Casey.
    p. cm.
ISBN 978-1-55725-460-3
1. Benedict, Saint, Abbot of Monte Cassino. Regula.
2. Benedictines—Rules. I. Title.
BX3004.Z5C339 2005
255'.106—dc22   2005010809

10 9 8 7 6 5 4 3 2 1

Published by Paraclete Press
Brewster, Massachusetts
www.paracletepress.com
Printed in the United States of America

In memory of
Helen Lombard
1936 – 2000
Sister of the Good Samaritan
A Lover of the Rule

Contents

Preface

When monks and nuns commit themselves entirely to God in the solemn act of monastic profession it is as though they change their citizenship. Now they are citizens of heaven, living in an extraterritorial outpost that medieval authors termed the "cloistral paradise." Monastic living is, however, more than a question of location. Beyond prolonged residence in the place, commitment is demanded. This, in turn, implies more than mere punctiliousness in obeying the laws and observing local customs. It asks us to take on a new identity and to be reshaped according to a different culture. This refashioning must come from within. It cannot be superimposed by external pressure on an otherwise recalcitrant individuality. From the very beginning the candidate to monastic life is asked to consent to a different world-view, where previous priorities are turned upside down and a lifelong process of unlearning, learning, and relearning is initiated.

The transformation that occurs in monasteries is God's work, and no human effort can bring it about. Nevertheless it is a work in which the monk or nun has a role to play. There is an active phase in monastic growth where much effort needs to be expended. St. Benedict envisages the monk as a good tradesman, persevering in his task and making use of whatever implements are required to perform it well. In Chapter 4 he lists no less than seventy-three implements to be found in the monastic workshop—some of them more important than others, but all available should the need arise. The skilled worker is one who is able to recognize when a particular implement is called for and has the ability to use it appropriately.

In this book I am going to reflect on a number of the monastic means to holiness that I find in the *Rule of St. Benedict* and that to me seem particularly relevant not only to monasteries but to the Church as a whole. What Benedict presents to us is no more than a digest of gospel teaching applied to a particular situation. I hope to reflect on his words in a way that will enable you, the reader, to apply this doctrine to your own circumstances and perhaps find in the ancient writings words that are life-giving.

The key idea of this book is expressed in its title. Benedict advises his monks "to make themselves strangers to the actions of the age"—to become strangers to the city. This is done first by living somewhat apart, morally more than physically. The purpose of this "separation from the world" is to facilitate a distinctive lifestyle, based on distinctive premises and priorities. It must be obvious, moreover, that the maintenance of this particular way of life depends on an infrastructure of beliefs and values: Without personal convictions monastic living is no more than a pious charade. The monastic sub-culture, like every other, includes a good measure of theory as well as practice. Apart from this theory monastic living lacks integrity and is liable to exhaust itself in mindless virtue. There is, as has often been said, nothing so practical as good theory.

Most monastic people understand that the realistic living of monastic life (or *conversatio*) demands more than doing good and avoiding evil. It asks for a progressive and substantial change in attitude. We have constantly to take on board new beliefs and values, and submit to question some aspects of the philosophy of life we have built since our youth. This is the ongoing conversion that is demanded of us: more and more to view things with the eyes of Christ and to leave behind the self-serving individualism that has become our regular mainstay in thought and action.

This is a program of life so demanding that we readily seek meritorious distractions from its severity. We must beware. If we indulge in too much escapist behavior our whole life becomes fuzzy and we lose a sense of its direction. It is much better to be clear about what life is meant to be even when we fall far short of our ideal. That way, and with God's grace, we keep trying and, perhaps, with the passage of time our hearts become purer and our lives simpler. At least that is the way it is supposed to be!

The service rendered to the Church by fervent followers of St. Benedict is their stable and persevering effort to live lives shaped by the gospel. They aspire to create in the common microcosm of the monastery a miniature church where the universal struggle of divine grace and human sinfulness is played out. Only the outsider can perceive which way the battle is going. The insider is aware mainly of the grim reality of weakness and precariousness on every side. Hope in the victory of Christ is not yet seen, but clung to in faith.

In this book I am inviting you to enter with me into the monastic experience where, as in your own experience, life and death contend. Your experience will not be the same as mine. I am a male, a monk, an Australian, and probably in the final quadrant of my life. I speak as one formed in a specifically Cistercian approach to the Rule. Chances are that your CV scarcely overlaps with mine. That could be an asset. What I see from my vantage point is probably different from what you see from yours. With a bit of effort a fusion of horizons may occur so that from these pages you might see something in the Rule that you did not notice previously. I hope that a fuller contact with the life-enriching vision of St. Benedict will be a means of greater access to the evangelical wisdom that he taught through his Rule and through the form of monastic living that he established.

This book started life as an address given to a gathering of the *Communio Internationalis Benedicinarum* on 14 September 2003. It was published in *Tjurunga* 66 (2004), pp. 34–47. Since then the material has been workshopped with various monastic groups around the world. I am very grateful to all who have given me feedback and encouraged me to keep expanding the topic.

Michael Casey
11 July–25 December 2004

1 | *Distinctiveness*

> To *make oneself a stranger to*
> the actions of this age
> RB 4:20

St. Benedict finds those who are to become his followers in the midst of the multitude of people (Prol. 14), but in calling them to undertake the journey to the kingdom (Prol. 21), he necessarily invites them to come out from that multitude. Henceforth "this world" or, better, "this age"—Benedict uses *saeculum* rather than *mundus*—becomes a symbol of apostasy. "This age" and all its works are what we have left behind in following our vocation.[1] What is beyond the monastic sphere of influence is not good for our souls (66:7), it is destruction (*destructio*: 67:5). The danger, however, is not the world outside, as it were the Goths at the gates, but the world brought inside the monastery in the heads and hearts of monks and nuns.

It seems to me that the first and foremost call that comes to us today from Benedict's Rule is to become what we are meant to be. To embrace whole-heartedly our Benedictine and monastic identity, and to assert our distinctiveness in respect of "this age," the ambient culture that espouses so very few of the values that characterize our seeking of God. Our citizenship and *conversatio* are heavenly (Phil. 3:20).

Despite the fact that a previous Abbot Primate has stated that Benedict "has no place for *fuga mundi,*"[2] it is only by keeping a certain distance from society that we can hope to have some positive impact on it. The Gospel images of salt and leaven are reminders to us that our influence depends on our being different, on our remaining faithful to our vocation to be distinctive. "Salt is a good thing, but if salt becomes unsalty, how can you season it?" (Mk. 9:50). Abbot Parry pungently restates this ancient idea.

> The need to break visibly with the ways of the world, and to assert something more definitely by one's life-style, becomes more and more urgent as our society plunges morally into the abyss, and socially into disruption. The need is for witnesses whose witness is both intelligible and unmistakable, for witnesses who know how to reject and rebuke evil however disguised, and likewise proclaim what is good.[3]

This assertion of identity must be more than mere "contempt for the world," although some may believe that today there is much in many societies that is contemptible. It must derive from a certain clarity about our ultimate ideal and our goals, and also about the means necessary if we are to form succeeding generations so that they have some chance of persevering in their quest for God.[4]

1. Why Are You Here?

The first question Benedict addresses to a prospective disciple concerns motivation. "Friend, for what purpose have you come?" (RB 60:3). Oddly, it is almost the same challenge that Jesus put to Judas in the garden of Gethsemane (Mt. 26:50). A similar question is repeated in the ritual of monastic initiation: *Quid petis?* "For what do you seek?" Today, when this query is made of those who are attracted to the monastic way, many different responses are given depending on how extensive has been the candidate's exposure to the appropriate theological vocabulary. The replies are not necessarily insincere, but very often they reflect only what is happening at a conscious level. These overt aspirations do not always reveal the deeper drives that have brought candidates to the monastery door. It may be years later, sometimes only as they end their monastic career, that such persons become somewhat aware of the hidden motivations that were subtly influencing the choices they made.

Over recent decades there has been some evolution in the reasons given for wanting to enter a monastery. In the past, monastic life was seen as offering a chance to do penance for sins committed or, alternatively, for those whose lives were less blameworthy, the opportunity to make reparation for the sins of the world. There was also the idea of making intercession through the multiplication of prayers, good works, and acts of self-denial, and much reference was made to the "hidden apostolate" of contemplatives, in terms drawn from Pius XI's much-quoted letter to the Carthusians, *Umbratilem*. Others were initially attracted by the various services offered by particular monasteries, and wanted to participate in such sacred utility. Despite the acclaim offered to the "witness value" of monastic life, I do not know that this was an ideal that drew people into joining. More subtle motivations also operated: an attraction to the monastic ambiance, the good example of particular members of the community, or books read that lit a fire. In this last instance, it is well known that many were drawn to Cistercian monasticism by the writings of Thomas Merton.

At a deeper level, most genuine candidates find themselves somewhere on a continuum between uncomprehending obedience to the perceived will of God and the hope that monasticism will be for them a path to self-realization. Becoming aware of a "vocation" happens in many ways: Sometimes the call seems to be in continuity with a previous life, sometimes a "conversion" is demanded and a new beginning made. To some extent most of those who present themselves at the door of the monastery are fired by a vision of a misty alternative future—they see monastic life as a means to fulfilling their ultimate potential, as it were realizing their destiny. In this connection many older people used to speak about religious life as a means of "seeking the way to perfection."

Whatever brings a person to embrace the monastic way, it is unlikely to be sufficient for a lifetime. The transition into monasticism usually causes a degree of regression: Entrants may find themselves without the support of their carefully cultivated persona and, for a while, may wallow in the confusion of childish reactions.[5] The reality of community life brings to the surface many hidden needs and dynamics. Very quickly, a more searching motivation will be needed to assure survival.

Monastic life is not really about self-realization, in the immediate sense of these words: It is more about self-transcendence. These are noble words, but the reality they describe is a lifetime of feeling out of one's depth: confused, bewildered, and not a little affronted by the mysterious ways of God. This is why those who persevere and are buried in the monastic cemetery can rarely be described as perfectly integrated human beings. Far from it. We live and mostly die with our imperfections intact. Accepting this means letting go of efforts to manage one's self-definition and to control events in accordance with it. It means living in the insecurity of God's mercy and that of the community.

Self-transcendence is a relentlessly grinding process. It makes each one of us the anti-hero in the drama of our own life: unknowing, incompetent, bumbling. To persevere in such an unpoetic existence requires unusual skills, if they may be so called, and strong motivation. If persons are unaware of why they have decided to orient their lives in a particular direction, it will be very difficult for them to keep discerning the choices that further this endeavor.

This is why one of the early tasks confronting newcomers to monastic life is to understand by what dynamism Providence has led them to take this step. Once this has been done, they can sit back and wait for their newly crafted vision to fall apart. Then they can start again, re-assembling the pieces, with God's help, into an approach that will serve them for another few years. And so the process of re-definition continues. Even St. Bernard, we are told, used frequently to muse on his motives, as though to suggest that initial inspirations are not always sufficient to carry us through the variety of experiences by which our life is continually and creatively reconstituted.

Today, probably more than ever, entering a monastery is a major transition. Nobody slips unthinkingly into monastic life for the lack of a better alternative. Too many obstacles are encountered both before entry and in the years that follow it. We have to be very solidly convinced that we are following the right course, and our wills must be fully fixed on a distant goal. Monastic life is the diametric opposite of aimless living. It has a goal and it has a tried and ordered network of means by which that goal is realized. The train is running on tracks to a single destination; if you don't want to go there, you had better get off at the next stop.

The crucial issue for people involved in the monastic enterprise is finality. What is its ultimate purpose? Where is it leading? The goal of monastic life needs to be decided before any discussion about suitable means of attaining it. It is the end that renders the means meaningful. The question of goal is one addressed by John Cassian in his first *Conference*. His response is well-known. The monk aims, above all, for the kingdom of God. But his more immediate ambition is to rid his heart of complexity so that he seeks that goal in simplicity and without mixed motives. His most pressing task, therefore, is purity of heart. This means he uses anything that reduces the level of inner division. He embraces a disciplined lifestyle, he allows many of his options to be decided by others, he opens his heart to an experienced mentor, he submits in faith to the providential disturbances that he meets on his journey. As he makes progress, invisible though it is to himself, he connects more completely with the most purifying power of them all, the inward action of the Holy Spirit. By this peculiar conjunction of divine grace and human struggle, transformation occurs.

Those who embrace the monastic means as the determining elements in their behavior gradually acquire a new identity. This is something that grows from within. It is not a role played for whatever reason. It is not a temporary phase that will soon be abandoned. This monastic identity accompanies monks and nuns wherever they go, whatever they do. Sometimes this homing instinct points out to them life-giving byways and, when (not if) they go astray, it serves as a beacon to guide them back to integrity. But there is a choice to be made. Long before such an identity is formed, those who enter the monastic way are obliged to reorient their lives radically. According to ancient usage, the first step in becoming a monk is conversion.

2. Making the Break

Benedict calls his followers, as we have said, to come out from the multitude. This is how it is with every monastic vocation. We are born into a family, a culture, and an ambiance, and our attitudes are largely shaped by those with whom we have had contact. By and large, our priorities are not so different from those of our peers and contemporaries. Our future is relatively predictable based on our social class, our character and talents, our education. With each passing year the possibilities narrow. For most of us the announcement of a monastic interest caused surprise and shock to those who thought they knew us. What they did not know was that something had been happening deep inside us that impelled us to evaluate issues differently, and to turn aside from the future that others so confidently predicted for us.

What was this inner earthquake? Most of us would have found it hard to describe—at the time we were not so familiar with our interior landscape that we could easily discourse about it. We lacked a vocabulary adequate to convey our experience. Its component elements seemed trivial and banal—too insubstantial to bear the weight of their eventual consequences. When we think of conversion experiences we often imagine something dramatic happening as it did to St. Paul on the Damascus road. Yes, some conversions seem to be sudden, but often upon investigation we discover that the process had been brewing over a long period. It is only when the gathering force suddenly ruptures the shell of habit and erupts into ordinary life to change it irreversibly, that we see it. But it had long been working its magic underground.[6]

The principal and permanent effect of this inner experience was to bring about a change in our perceptual horizons. This is to say that we began to see issues in a different light. We were no longer under the full thrall of appearances, but we had begun to glimpse something of the reality underlying human affairs. The more clearly we saw, the more differently we evaluated possibilities. Once we made the radical choice to submit to this secret summons, we now questioned goals and assumptions that previously seemed routine, and a great ferment resulted. We had a sense that we were being impelled toward a different future, though we did not always know clearly what shape that future would assume.

Because the world looked different, it slowly became clear that a different lifestyle was demanded of us. There may have been elements of guilt and shame about our past, but the primary feeling was one of joy and exhilaration. This made us bold in confronting negativity in our own life and around us. Often we were overly severe on ourselves and others at this phase. It was easier to reject what was obviously dissonant with our new dream than to know what might lead to its realization. Only with the passing of time and, perhaps, the waning of enthusiasm did realistic possibilities begin to open up before us. None of them was a perfect fit, but one stood out as offering a skeleton around which a new self could be formed.

And so we came to the monastery.

3. Frontiers

Few of us will ever forget the day we crossed the monastic threshold to begin a new life. It was a solemn moment of entering a new environment and leaving behind much of what had become second nature to us. It was almost like a new birth. We were infants, unable to predict or control what would happen next, feeling that our presence contributed little to the functioning of this well-oiled machine, constantly wondering whether we had made the right decision.

As we recovered from that initial sense of displacement we discovered a whole new world of strangeness. The monastery operated on principles different from those to which we were accustomed. We found a community strong on antique ritual and symbolism and often indifferent to fashion and efficiency and somewhat removed from the banalities of suburban concern and conversation. At a deeper level our conviction that cause and effect were related seemed challenged at ever turn. Things happened without apparent reason, not only in the petty details of daily life, but even at important junctures of spiritual development. Perhaps with a rising panic we became aware that in a monastery we would never be in control—especially if we happened to become a superior. Underlying the reasonable and ordered facade was a frothy chaos that seemed ever on the point of overwhelming the community, but in fact never did. Our own identity too was in a state of flux. The primacy of self had been displaced, and there did not seem much to take its stead. Especially at the beginning, but, for some, sporadically through life, we seemed to be living in a foreign country. In the monastic world we felt ourselves as resident aliens. At times like this we may have been surprised to feel a little homesick and experience a certain nostalgia for the life we had abandoned with so much alacrity.

It is important to recognize that the abnormality of the monastic lifestyle is not a mere accident of recent history. Certain aspects of it may be unduly quaint or archaic, but the corporate lifestyle as a whole needs to be different from that of normal society "outside" because it embodies and expresses different beliefs and values. Individual members are supported and formed in living their distinctive philosophy not so much by intense personal direction as by participation in the common life, the common work, and the network of common relationships that together constitute the community. By being with others of the same persuasion, by acting in concert with them and by permitting the free flow of thought and feeling, we absorb the community identity. Simultaneously we become more ourselves, not in isolation, but ourselves in relation with others.

We live in a period in which religious practice is becoming progressively more privatized and more the object of personal choice. It is sometimes hard to give up the idea of a designer religion, in which everything is tailored to my present needs and aspirations. Delivering oneself into the hands of a community of relative strangers and asking to be formed does not seem like a very good idea. Yielding control does not come easily to me; I don't always appreciate the fact that self-transcendence is impossible so long as the self remains in the driver's seat. Even if I can learn to discern the difference between life-giving choices and those that lead nowhere, I am still bedeviled by deeper impulses that so often guide my actions but escape the scrutiny of my conscious mind. Even the most sincerely pious searchers after God harbor within themselves much hazardous material that, if disregarded, may eventually poison their best efforts. The fact that so many of our contemporaries do not recognize is that the higher our religious aspirations, the more we need the guidance and support of other people. If we intend merely to coast along the low roads, maybe we can do it alone. If we are heading for the mountains, the support of others is indispensable.

The lifestyle of the community we entered is not simply the sum total of individual neuroses. It is a community that stands in a tradition that has perdured for a millennium and a half. The basic parameters of the lifestyle, which no "Benedictine" can abandon, have their constitutional basis in the Rule of Benedict. Although Benedict is open to other input, his basic insight is that this fundamental law of community life is to be interpreted and applied by those who have experience in living it and the capacity to communicate this experience to others. No priority is given to bright ideas. Everything has to be measured against experience. The result can sometimes seem a bit stodgy, as we fail to keep up with the latest trends. The monastic tradition is so extensive that it does not give itself to easy maneuverability, but there is something solid about it. Its very archaism can serve to protect us from fads and "novelties" that hold sway for a season and then disappear. The rhythms of the monastic day are dictated by specific monastic goals; they do not have to conform to the preferences of those who seek something else.

It is important to note, at this juncture, that accepting to live monastic *conversatio* is not a matter of going back to live in a previous century. It is much more radical than that.

The sixth century has no more claim on us than our own. Benedict does not recommend his own century to us, he teaches us to leave it behind and to try something different. We are citizens of heaven, and, knowing this, we try to live in accordance with heavenly standards as these are conveyed to us in the Gospels.

4. Benedict's Contribution

As far as we can make his acquaintance, Benedict seems like an attractive person—much more so than the Master, for instance. But we need to respect his historical distinctiveness. We need to beware of turning him into a glove puppet spouting the preferred platitudes of our own generation. We should not attempt to co-opt Benedict as the spokesman for our twenty-first-century agenda. He is his own man. And he is not slow to make solid demands of those who would become his followers.

The community as envisaged by Benedict does not operate according to the standards of this age. Many of us would find his provisions too severe and unyielding. While it is true that Benedict is sensitive to weakness, he expects the "strong" to pull their weight and maintain a solid degree of monastic observance. Some of his precepts seem unreasonably hard to us. But Benedict is convinced that this apparent harshness is the way that leads to God (58:8) by blocking the tyranny of self-will, making provision for the extinguishment of vices and giving scope for the flowering of love (Prol. 47).

Let us look at some of the texts that we find hard, distasteful, or difficult to understand. Benedict resists any tendency which would lead his monks to do any of the following:

- to be more concerned about "transitory earthly trifles" than the kingdom (2:33–36),

- to become protective of private property (33:1–8, 55:16–18),
- to be pleased to receive gifts (54:1–5),
- to be responsive to hospitality when traveling (51:1-2),
- to be happy to make extra profit from their work (57:7-8),
- to be hopeful for an inheritance (59:6),
- to pay attention to worldly rank (2:18),
- to insist on clerical privilege (60:5–7),
- to be prejudiced in favor of blood relatives (69:2),
- to claim the right to grumble when things go against them (5:17-18, 34:6-7, 40:9),
- to remain enthralled by self-congratulation (*elatio*: 4:69),
- to engage in self-promotion (*exaltatio*: 7:2, 7:7),[7]
- to keep their options open (58:15-16),
- to indulge in laughter (6:8, 7:59),
- to exercise initiative (31:4, 49:9, 67:7),
- to eat more than sparingly (39:7–10)[8] and
- to want to bathe frequently (36:8).

Most of these actions would be considered normal behavior in secular society—and, indeed, they may seem harmless enough. They become reprehensible only in the context of the holy community that Benedict is establishing—the school of the Lord's service, to recall the phrase with which we are all familiar. In such a lifestyle there are new demands because there is a substantial discontinuity with the manner of living evidenced all around us. Benedict is establishing a second and more specific level of morality. This is why actions and attitudes that are "unmonastic" such as laughter, grumbling, and drinking to satiety, evoke from him a greater wrath than those that are merely immoral. That is why the complex of attitudes

Benedict collects under the umbrella of "humility" makes little sense and holds little appeal outside the context of a fervent commitment to the monastic ideal.

Such provisions are not mere archaism to be explained away and abandoned without regret. They are indications that Benedict's community lives according to norms different from those typical of "this age." Chronological inculturation and *aggiornamento* are fine unless they begin to undermine the radical distinctiveness of monastic *conversatio*. In the process of updating of monastic life it is important that we seek not only new ways of relating to the age in which we live, but also new ways of expressing our essential distinctiveness.

There will always be a problem in deciding where to locate the boundaries between the monastery and the world. Within the Benedictine tradition there have been many different solutions accepted by different groups and yielding good results. If the monastery is to develop a nurturing and creative sub-culture it seems that some balance needs to be achieved between distinctiveness and porosity. I am not recommending constructing a cultural chasm between ourselves and the age in which we live. Nor do I believe this to have been Benedict's intention. But we need sufficient distance to generate the freedom to create our own enculturated sub-culture. Too much "openness" can lead to a loss of symbols, a decline in morale, and maybe eventually to near-indistinguishability. Walls that are too impermeable, on the other hand, can lead to the creation of a "social fantasy system" in which reality "inside" begins to have more weight than reality "outside," and people are hurt. Defining appropriate frontiers is an area where discernment is especially vital.

Before we arrive at the point of legislating for material separation, it is necessary to ensure that there is a more fundamental differentiation. In the chapters that follow we will explore different aspects of a monastic outlook that define and identify the followers of St. Benedict.

2 | *Asceticism*

To deny oneself to oneself
in order to follow Christ
RB 4:10

Monasticism without renunciation is meaningless. The greedy, lazy, and self-indulgent monk is a figure of fun in many medieval stories. Wherever we find genuine monasticism, there is an emphasis on a simple, austere way of life in which normal human desires are but scantily fulfilled. Monks serve as a reminder that a life of ease and pleasure is not the best way to find ultimate fulfillment. In a Christian setting those who practise monastic renunciation point to the existence of a richer and fuller life beyond death in eternity.

Benedict recognizes that implementing the attraction to pursue the way that leads to life (Prol. 20) necessarily involves discipline and renunciation. John Cassian's third *Conference* clearly sets forth an experiential teaching that shows how the different levels of renunciation are woven into the very texture of monastic life. Without some channeling of energies there is no possibility of attaining the goals that monasticism places before itself. "He is badly deceived who thinks that while he lives in this mortal body that he has no need of bodily exercises."[9] Following Christ is impossible without shouldering his cross. It does not take much observation to come to the conclusion that systematic lack of renunciation is the root cause of many familiar situations of malaise, signaled by narcissistic attitudes, tepidity, behavior inconsistent with monastic profession, a chronic tendency to conflict, acedia, or a generalized lack of commitment.

Finality is crucial. Practices that involve the curtailment of desire have never been enjoyable. Any approach to life that would recommend such an approach to life must be anathema especially to an age in which self-gratification is seen as the normal mode of human existence. Although sexual abstinence, sleep-deprivation, fasting, poverty, and various forms of austerity are widely attested among ascetical groups in all the world religions, mere statistical support is not enough to encourage people to undertake them. Only a bent disposition would renounce gratification and choose suffering unless some proportionate advantage could be expected. If the pain leads to gain, there is no problem. Champion athletes and professionals in every sphere of life understand that purpose-driven renunciation is essential in any pursuit of excellence. Most are not motivated to asceticism if they cannot see any purpose in it. Finality is crucial; there must be a purpose in mortification.

> "Asceticism is necessary first of all for creative action of any kind, for prayer, for love: in other words, it is needed by each of us throughout our entire life. . . . *Every Christian is an ascetic.*" Without asceticism none of us is authentically human.[10]

In inculcating the values of the ascetic life, it is necessary that we are able to demonstrate their finality: We fast, we obey, we are celibate, for this reason or for that, not because it is the rule or the tradition, but because it is perceived to produce good effects in our life.[11] The fact that we sometimes find it difficult to come up with convincing reasons for many customary observances may indicate that our own values may need deepening. The much-chronicled loss of the sense of sin[12] has effectively invalidated penance as a motivation, since the link between personal guilt and penitential practices has been considerably weakened. For many people, even for those who embrace monastic life, this reluctance is not so much due to a lack of generosity or fervor, but derives from a general inability to understand why denying pleasure to myself can be a benefit to me or to anyone else.

One approach is to emphasize the cenobitic forms of self-restraint. By limiting my level of self-gratification I make fewer demands on others in the community. I appropriate less of the common resources. I am available to be at the service of brothers or sisters and to play second fiddle to their virtuoso performances. Probably I will be friendlier and more cooperative in general, more manageable in work situations and less competitive on less structured occasions. I can be reasonably sure that nobody in my community would complain if I become less self-gratifying. For those of an altruistic disposition, this rationale can work well. For others it can sometimes lead to the querulous plaint, "Why should I be the one always to deny myself? What about me?"

The approach taken by Abba Paphnutius in Cassian's third *Conference* is more direct. He sees three levels of renunciation in the life of the monk.

a) By the first renunciation he departs from family and possessions and embraces the monastic lifestyle.

b) By the second renunciation, which engages his energies for most of his life, he struggles to find freedom from the slavery of his past life and the vices of both body and spirit.

c) The third renunciation allows him so fully to let go of this familiar world that he is drawn into the sphere of the spirit and begins to experience here on earth the reality of heavenly bliss.

Beginning at the end, as the first *Conference* recommends, he recognizes that the goal of monastic life is to arrive at that singleness of outlook that permits the experience of God. For this to happen, the monk has to confront, and by grace to overcome, the instincts and tendencies that complicate his life and muddy the surface of his mind. This is difficult to achieve so long as he is embroiled in the inevitable turmoil associated with family and career. So he abandons a normal existence, makes an effort to live as a monk, and after years of undramatic struggle comes to a point of self-transcendence where the spiritual world begins to form part of his everyday horizon. At this final stage the work begun in initial conversion finds its completion. The purpose of renunciation is clear in such a long-term perspective. It is the means by which a monk prepares himself to be drawn into the contemplation of God. If you want to see God then attain purity of heart: If you want an undivided heart then live a simple life—and that involves systematically eliminating whatever makes it unnecessarily complex. In other words, it involves renunciation. So long as we live fragmented existences any pursuit of contemplative experience is likely to be frustrated. This is what Thomas Merton says with his usual trenchancy.

> The first thing you have to do before you set about thinking about such a thing as contemplation is to try to recover your basic natural unity, to reintegrate your compartmentalized being into a coordinated and single whole, and learn to live as a unified human person. This means that you have to bring back together the fragments of

your distracted existence so that when you say
"I" there is really someone present to support the
pronoun you have uttered.[13]

Those who seek the guidance of Hindu and Buddhist
spiritual masters seem to manifest a certain willingness to
accept a stern discipline of life as a means of entering more
deeply into meditation. They do not always grasp the connection between asceticism and mysticism, but they believe
that their confidence in their spiritual guide is well-placed. As
a result they practise renunciation, they are open to guidance,
they accept criticism and correction. In Zen meditation
halls those whose attention wavers are brought back to
concentration by a sharp blow on the neck with a stick. If we
tried that in the West we would probably end up in jail!

Christian mystical tradition is no less equipped to guide
people in the way of prayer, but for some reason we seem
less bold in making demands on those who seek instruction.
In the past few centuries these techniques (if they may be so
called) are more psychological than physical or bodily.
There is less adventure involved in the examination of
conscience or learning to practise meekness than in fasting
or shaving one's head. It may be that the credibility of the
Church is less, not only because of scandals, but also due
to the fact that its representatives are sometimes perceived
as part of an institutional power structure and therefore
resented. Too many years of fund-raising, building construc-
tion, liturgical management, and social involvement may
have engineered such an extroverted image of the clergy
that some may become dubious about their competence
in matters of interiority. Those who are looking for "something more" veer towards the exotic, not always wisely.
Another possible reason is more theological. Especially since
the Second Vatican Council, our emphasis on grace and on
the mercy of God can sometimes lead us to see less clearly
the role that the practice of intelligent discipline plays in

neutralizing vice and preparing the way for contemplative experience.

The mystical tradition of the West is no lame duck. It is clear both about its goals and the means that are necessary to attain them. We can find plenty of evidence to support this assertion by leaping back a few centuries and looking at the way Benedict approached asceticism and how he integrated it in a tradition that remained true to itself without disregarding the human needs of those who sought to be guided by it.

1. St. Benedict's Approach to Asceticism

The way of life established by the Rule of Benedict does not give much scope for dramatic feats of ascetical practice. In fact the standard of living, the level of comfort, and the availability of conveniences may appear to be somewhat higher than that of the average family in the locality. It takes a little experience to perceive the strictness that more often than not underlies the veneer of gracious living.

a) Benedictine Asceticism Consists in Corporate Living.

The choice of individual mortification can sometimes be spoiled by inappropriate motivation and self-will. Very often people will be attracted to practices that reinforce their vices rather than neutralize them. One who is overly taciturn will aim at becoming even more silent, and another who has anorexic tendencies may manifest a zest for fasting. Choosing exactly the wrong means is a proclivity well chronicled in Gregory the Great's *Pastoral Rule*. This is why Benedict does not want his monks to burden themselves with extra practices during Lent unless they first check matters out with the spiritual father (49:8–10). To the incurable individualist, self-denial is no longer much fun if everybody is doing it. In addition, control of the exercise passes out of one's own hands. My experience in some communities would lead me to conclude that it can be more penitential to eat the common meal than to abstain. Certainly this was often the case in twelfth-century Cistercian monasteries where miracles were sometimes necessary to make the food digestible. If the great enemy to spiritual growth is self-will, then the most effective means of progress is to curtail its exercise. Following the common norm in all things without murmuring or self-inflation is probably one of the best means of doing this.

b) Benedictine Asceticism is Being Subject to Discernment.

Having a goal means that there is always a standard against which every proposition can be measured. Adopting a disciplined lifestyle means that a certain lightness and spontaneity is lost. Whatever course of action a monk seeks to follow, whatever plan a community adopts, must be submitted to the test of whether the proposition is likely to contribute to the realization of the fundamental purpose of monastic life. Inevitably there are different views about such matters, and the eventual decision may go against my personal preferences. There is an asceticism involved in consenting to live a life based on principles and values rather than on whatever captivates me at a particular moment. It means that there is no chance of relief, no vacation. All my days are passed under a discipline that depends on interior attitudes rather than on external regulation. This is the way of life I have chosen; this is how I express who I am. Unfortunately I can never have a holiday from myself. Sometimes we will find ourselves hankering for a more mindless existence.

c) Benedictine Asceticism Adapts to Circumstances.

St. Benedict is praised for his flexibility. He gives the abbot the right to change or suspend any measure that is not working because of particular circumstances. There is, however, a flip side to this admirable quality. The abbot is expected to cool things down in favor of the "weak," but he is also instructed to turn up the heat when he is dealing with the "strong" (64:19). This attitude means that there is less danger of asceticism being reduced to the level of the institutional and symbolic. If there is no bite in daily monasticism, there is a possibility that monks and nuns will forget what they are about, and devote most of the waking hours to concern about work, relationships, and practical matters. The search has ceased. Desire for God has become submerged, cocooned under a mountain of immediate concerns. If life here below is too comfortable we will want to settle down. Where a sense of purpose fails, morale plummets. Asceticism reminds us that we are not yet in heaven, we are still on the way. It invites us to lift up our hearts to where our treasure is, and to find our principal joy there.

d) Benedictine Asceticism is Moderate.

Again, the moderation of Benedict is rightly celebrated. Moderation and sufficiency are the principles that guide his ordering of daily life: Extremism and excess are eliminated. For all who give themselves to lifelong fidelity to the Rule, this is a valuable protection against early burnout. Surprisingly, however, moderation is not so easy to observe. Sometimes it is easier to go without than to walk the fine line between too much and too little. The point about Benedict's provisions is that no single observance is absolutized. Abstemiousness in food gives way to the special needs that follow manual work (41:4-5); the great silence after compline can be broken on behalf of guests (42:10), and loving consideration is to be shown to old men and children (37:3).

e) Benedictine Asceticism is Unremitting.

"The life of the monk should have a Lenten character all the time" (49:1). The vow of stability means that the monk is deprived of the possibility of disguising his lack of commitment by moving around. Despite the fact that Benedict recognizes that few have the strength to live in a perpetual Lent, and he himself was rebuked for attempting to do so, the ideal remains. A monk expects that the value of self-denial will have some scope in his daily experience; if it has dropped off the radar of his conscience, something is wrong. The paradox one often encounters in fervent communities is that the level of asceticism often rises as the years go by. Austerity of life is not something imposed on newcomers to channel their fervor, but it is a choice that grows out of inner conviction as a monk learns to embrace with delight and from the love of Christ things that may hitherto have seemed hard and burdensome (Prol. 47-48, 7:68-69). The principle of self-denial as a means of discipleship remains intact until one's final breath, though obviously the means used will vary according to possibility.

f) Benedictine Asceticism is Invisible.

Those with a superficial acquaintance with monastic communities often come to the conclusion that Benedictine *conversatio* is not so tough. It is true that the more dramatic austerities of former times are no longer much in evidence: There is less silence, the food is better, the hours of sleep are longer, and the exclusion of the modern world is less total. These are only minor adaptations. The great struggle against self is not fought on these fronts. It takes place more at the level of maintaining one's personal commitment as one changes and the world and the monastery also change. Stability is not a matter of inertly standing still, but like riding on a surfboard, it demands a lot of effort to stay up. Living in the same place, with the same people, and following the same rule of life for forty years and more is a particular challenge in our times; the tendency to escape either physically or mentally is strong. This is why the hardest thing of all for many today is staying put and letting the monastic process run through to completion. We are far too inclined to believe that if immediate gratification is lacking it is because something is wrong and change is called for. Wrong! Patience is called for, as Benedict seems to have recognized (Prol. 50), until we get to the point where things get easier and sometimes seem quite delightful.

Benedict's program of renunciation (if it may be so termed) is built upon the conception of a community formed by gospel values, a group of people who declare their independence of the society in which they live by choosing different priorities. It is not primarily negative. Those who faithfully follow Benedict's Rule are not usually fiercely world-rejecting, body-denying, self-hating people. They are not fanatics. Those formed by monastic tradition more often than not come out the other end as prudent, gentle, and tolerant, both toward themselves and toward others.

2. Giving Primacy to Interiority

A particular area of asceticism that is characteristic of the Benedictine tradition is summarized in the word often chosen to epitomize it: *Peace.* Elsewhere I have written of monastic *conversatio* as "an unexciting life." Ideally it makes prudent use of a technique recently given the acronym REST, "Restricted Environmental Stimulation."[14] Most of us live in a sensate culture with a vast appetite for the sensational. As a result many young people find monastic life "boring," and many of the not-so-young welcome any drama to break the tedium of a typical monastic day. More than twenty years ago I coined the phrase "creative monotony." Today, more than ever, I believe that this should be one of our important priorities: to make our communities places of intense peace, where interiority is possible and positive reinforcement is given to those who wish to journey deeper into prayer. This involves a certain enthusiasm for the discipline and practice of silence, non-communication, recollection. The purpose of a quiet life needs to be clear: It is to facilitate a quiet mind in which spiritual priorities become progressively more dominant. Nor is this withdrawal an invitation to isolation and introspection. It is, rather, a matter of providing the opportunity of entering more deeply into reality and of living from the heart. As prayer becomes less conceptual, however, there is a movement away from involvement in all sorts of busyness, yet without becoming less present to common and communal life. In fact, the lack of external stimulation has been seen in the tradition of Evagrius as one mode of apatheia, which, in turn, was regarded as the generator of agape.[15]

An interior life demands a reduction in the importance given to many external events—notably those ephemeral happenings that fill our newspapers today and are forgotten next week. It is also a move away from the elevation of all sorts of trivialities into issues of major importance. Often it is the renunciation of a tendency to create a tempest in a teacup and, instead, to choose the path of peacemaking. Above all, the way of interiority is the acceptance of spiritual poverty, a tolerance for the dark way of faith, and a take-it-or-leave-it attitude to all that is not God. Again, Thomas Merton says it well.

Contemplative prayer is, in a way, simply the preference for the desert, for emptiness, for poverty. One has begun to know the meaning of contemplation when [one] intuitively and spontaneously seeks the dark and unknown path of aridity in preference to every other way. The contemplative is one who would rather not know than know. Rather not enjoy than enjoy. Rather not have proof that God loves him.[16]

The key word seems to be "preference." Choosing a low-impact lifestyle as a means to living a more intense spiritual life is an option willingly pursued. It can never be imposed from without. A quiet life marked by periods of solitude and silence and characterized by patience and calmness cannot be created by external regulation. It can come only from a heart that has tasted how good the Lord is and how energizing it can be to be still before the Lord. To such a one the renunciation of many fatuous excitements is no hardship, but the highway to inner tranquility.

In all this we are confronted with a choice about whether we live from the heart or allow our lives to be dictated by what happens around us. Fundamental to any serious attempt to live a spiritual life is the priority given to the deep self over the superficial self. Living from the heart means negating self-will, refusing to allow the ego to dominate our affairs. Asceticism tries to put a bridle on the ego's wild impulses, to reduce the highs and lows of immature desire, and to bring some consistency and gravitas into our search for God. Part of how this is accomplished is the creation of an ambiance in which interior impulses are not only permitted but actively encouraged to assert themselves.

3 | *Leisure*

A disciple should be quiet and listen.
RB 6:6

The Benedictine vocation includes within its integrity an attraction to leisure—a time and space of freedom in which the deep self can find fuller expression.[17] In a paradoxical sense, self-realization is the principal task of the monk or nun in the Benedictine tradition. This is not the result of a self-conscious narcissism, but derives from a fundamental fidelity to God's call embodied in what we are, the imperative to allow full scope to the potentialities of our nature. That is why members of a community that follows Benedict's rule are such a varied lot. They are not formed by particular tasks to be accomplished, but are encouraged to grow to the limit of their particular possibilities in the tasks assigned to them. Practically, communities have to engage in work that provides for their support. Ideally, the money-making occupations of a monastic community do no more than finance a modest lifestyle together with the possibility of helping others. Work is not designed to maximize profit so as to enable conspicuous consumption. To some extent monastic work grows out of the possibilities presented by those who make up the community. If this happens, then work not only provides self-support, it also offers the possibility of self-expression and human fulfillment. It can become a channel of growth that forms the character of those involved in it. It is because monastics strive to be fully present in whatever occupation engages them that the work they do is endowed with a special character. Their work is shaped by pursuit of excellence that is typical of those who embrace the monastic way.

1. Leisure as Silence

Leisure is not idleness or the pursuit of recreational activities. It is, above all, being attentive to the present moment, open to all its implications, living it to the full. This implies a certain looseness in lifestyle that allows heart and mind to drift away from time to time. Monastic life is not a matter of shoehorning the maximum number of good works into a day. It is more important that monks and nuns do a few things well, being present to the tasks they undertake, leaving room for recuperation and reflection, and expecting the unexpected. Leisure allows openness to the present. It is the opposite of being enslaved by the past or living in some hazy anticipation of a desirable future. Leisure means being free from anything that would impede, color, or subvert the perception of reality. Far from being the headlong pursuit of escapist activities and having fun, authentic leisure is a very serious matter because it is the product of an attentive and listening attitude to life.

> Leisure is a form of silence which is the prerequisite of the apprehension of reality. Leisure is a receptive attitude of mind, a contemplative attitude, and it is not only the occasion but also the capacity for steeping oneself in the whole of creation.[18]

Benedict's monastery is a place of leisure because those who live there are committed to a life of mindfulness. Being attentive requires, first of all, that we renounce the desire to control what happens around us, to manipulate reality, to impose our will on events or on other people. We often think that those who try to keep control of everything around them are strong and domineering people, attempting to rule others and to mould them in their own likeness. Usually this is not so. Control-freaks are most often fearful people who are threatened by the prospect that events would be allowed to take an independent direction. Underneath the firm grip and the bluster is a wavering self-confidence that fears to face the unexpected. By constraining everything to squeeze itself into the hard shell of their expectations, they fail to read and respect the reality of the world around them. They are heedless of what is outside themselves because they are driven mercilessly by their own insecurity. Their life is a constant battle to prevent reality from asserting its independence. Their inner voices are shouting so loudly that they can hear nothing else.

We all need to learn the art of silence, to still the clamor that comes from within as well as securing for ourselves a zone where outward noise is sometimes hushed. Above all we need to teach ourselves to become somewhat more silent, because it is through an undisciplined tongue that much of our personal and social disturbance comes. In a world where communication is huge, it takes a fair amount of resolution to create for oneself a sphere of silence, in which external urgencies are put on hold and words are weighed. Just as it is important for us to make "quality time" for people we love, so we need to reserve some moments—and more than moments—for coming to an understanding of what is happening within us and around us. We will never have a listening attitude to life unless we spend time listening. That means we stop talking and we stop engaging in consciousness-absorbing activities and start paying attention. If we do this often enough, it may become semi-habitual.

Of course, such periods of silence and solitude have to be purchased at the expense of other activities, and that is what we do not like. We do not want to give up any of the elements that we have built into our lives, be they ever so trite and paltry. We have first to be convinced of the value of holy leisure. This is where a problem arises. Leisure is content-free; it is good in so far as it is filled with goodness, but it obviously has the capacity to be poisoned by malice. This is why there is, notably in Latin, a certain ambiguity about the term itself and a corresponding ambivalence towards the reality it describes. Leisure is empty space. We find it hard to make room for *nothing* in our crowded lives; like nature we abhor a vacuum. Better to do something useful, we say, than simply mope. A period of involuntary inactivity due to unforeseen circumstances we find very hard to endure.

> Silence, however, stands outside the world of profit and utility; it cannot be exploited for profit; you cannot get anything out of it. It is "unproductive." Therefore it is regarded as valueless. Yet there is more help and healing in silence than in all the "useful things." Purposeless, unexploitable silence suddenly appears at the side of the all-too-purposeful, and frightens us by its very purposelessness. It interferes with the regular flow of the purposeful. It strengthens the untouchable, it lessens the damage inflicted by exploitation. It makes things whole again, by taking them back from the world of dissipation into the world of wholeness. It gives something of its own holy uselessness, for that is what silence itself is: holy uselessness.[19]

Attentiveness is acquired by most people through a habit of reflectiveness—learning to step back from experience to ponder its meaning. Most often meaning presents itself to a gently disengaged consciousness—fierce interrogation habitually yields nothing. As Archimedes discovered, insights often come at the most unlikely moment. Those who give a high priority to the pursuit of wisdom should, accordingly, try to structure their lives so that times of disengagement are multiplied. This is not necessarily a matter of scheduling in high-powered periods of concentration; at least this is not Benedict's way. In the traditional ordering of the monastic day "intervals" were provided in which nothing much happened. Provision was made for the possibility of moving from one place or activity to another, for leaving aside a particular occupation and temporarily disengaging from its concerns. Leisure means living gently; it is the opposite of being driven or obsessed. It involves getting on with the job at hand and detaching oneself from it when it is time to move on to something else. To some extent leisure invites us to cultivate the virtue of inefficiency. We are far more likely to notice the scenery if we dawdle along the way than if we rocket along at mind-numbing speed. Leisure calls us to avoid the cumulative sense of incompletion that occurs when we find ourselves burdened with the weight of so many cares and unfinished tasks. It is a childlike concern only for the present. I suppose it was easier in a world not dominated by calendars and clocks simply to take each day as it comes. On the other hand, making the effort to overthrow the tyranny of time yields proportionately higher profits to those of us who try it sometimes. It is like a liberation. We have to realize, however, that the tyrant is inside us, not outside.

2. Room to Breathe

A community that embraces the ideal of leisure gives its members room to breathe. It is a gift of time and space. Time for oneself; time for one another; time to listen, encourage, and support; time to step back and discern, to assess the quality of actions; time to develop culture and ritual and good liturgy. Space for people to grow, space for different gifts, space for the stranger, space to pass through crises. A community that prizes leisure is more interested in persons than in the accomplishment of tasks; community activities are more about subjective meanings than simply a matter of getting work done. Leisure is, as Pope John Paul II has often insisted, about building a culture of humanization.

Any group that takes seriously the advantages of providing for its members an appropriate measure of freedom will stand out clearly in our purpose-driven world. The disciplined asceticism of the community is not designed to shepherd everybody into well-worn tracks and keep them there. It is intended to safeguard the integrity of each so that subjective forays into creativity are both true to self and harmonious within the communal setting. Leisure is one of the effects of an asceticism dedicated to promoting a fully human way of life. It deliberately moderates the inflow of external demands so that what is interior and personal is not swamped. This sounds great. It is not so easy to implement. We soon discover that the possibilities of escape from fully personal living are legion and attractive, and that it requires persevering effort to maintain mindfulness in a world that constantly summons us to distraction.

3. The Enemies of Leisure

The enemies of leisure attack from both sides. On the one hand we may be tempted to be more diligent and hard-working, on the other to take things easy and allow ourselves to drift at the behest of whatever influence dominates a particular moment. We are all familiar with persons who work too hard, who are obsessive, ambitious, or hyper-diligent, who take on too many jobs and never seem to reach a point when they are not preoccupied with what has to be done next. Such people experience little leisure. Other strangers to leisure are less visible. These are the slothful, those who lack commitment, those who seek means to insulate themselves from the demands of the present moment and, if possible, to escape from them. Such activities as they consent to do expand to fill all available time; there is never any possibility of undertaking anything extra. To the casual observer it may appear that the lazy person leads a more leisured life but, in reality, such a vacuous existence falls far short of the true meaning of leisure, because in their own minds there is never any room for an unexpected adventure.

Monks are often imagined to be lazy creatures. Mostly this is not true. More often than not their temptations come from the opposite direction. Consider this wonderful picture of an overworking monk in John Cassian's ninth conference.

> A certain very experienced elder once happened to be passing by the cell of a brother who was afflicted by an illness of the soul which caused him to toil at constructing and repairing buildings every day, far beyond what was necessary. From a distance the elder watched him breaking hard rock with a heavy hammer. Then he noticed an Ethiopian standing beside him also grasping the

hammer as he hit the rock, and who kept urging him on with fiery promptings to work harder.

The elder stood still for a long time, amazed at the sight of such a baleful demon, and at the extent of the deception being inflicted. When the brother became tired and had no energy left and wanted to put an end to the work and rest, then at the prompting of this spirit he was persuaded to take up the hammer again and encouraged not to desist from what he had intended to do when he began. The brother was so moved by these urgings that his tiredness left him and so he resumed the heavy work, and yet he felt no pain.

The elder saw what the hard-working brother did not: that his labors were not dictated by a reasoned judgment, but by the secret connivance of the demon. He was not a free man; he was a slave of the demon of overwork. The elder decided to intervene.

The elder was so disturbed by this performance on the part of the dread demon that he turned aside to the brother's cell and greeted him. "Brother, what is this work that you are doing," he asked. And the brother answered, "We are working on this very hard rock and it is only with great difficulty that we are able to make any impression on it." At this the old man replied, "It is well that you say 'We,' since you are not alone when you are working on the rock. There was another with you whom you did not see, who has been less a helper than a most oppressive taskmaster in this work."[20]

Cassian diagnoses the monk's problem as being "worldly ambition," which he defines curiously as "whatever contributes to our power," whatever makes us think that we can accomplish things by our own ingenuity and strength. There is, in other words, a connection between the spirit of leisure and the deliberate renunciation of power.

Despite appearances, compulsive overwork is more likely to be the outcome of vice than of virtue. Motivation is crucial. In the case of Cassian's monk, as with most good people like ourselves, unworthy motivations are usually hidden from us, but perfectly visible to others. More often than not, we do too much because we are afraid of being judged as failures, we do not trust others to do their share, we wish to exclude alternative approaches, or we want to ensure that we remain unchallenged in the driver's seat. Mostly, our perceptions are distorted. We have not taken time to see clearly. "Such a hard worker!" others say; but nobody thinks to ask why. All we know is that we feel good when we are on top of things; when projects slip away from our control we feel bad.

Potency is often delusional in that the euphoria it generates blinds us to anything but our own contribution to a task, our own importance in the general scheme of things. Meanwhile others may be unjustly exploited or undervalued. Power always works for its own benefit and increase. Smitten with blind ambition to expand into the realm of omnipotence, it never rests. There is no time to be still and admire, no time to wonder and be intrigued by paradox. It cannot afford to be surprised and to break out in cries of celebration. Language is tortured out of shape to prevent reality obtruding, sequential logic is lost, and the songs of poetry are stilled by the onrush of relentless self-serving verbiage.

A leisurely mind consists in being open to the wildness of universal reality. This means being content not to be in control—not seeking to stamp my trademark on everything around, permitting others to exercise autonomy in the imagination and execution of tasks. The result of this detachment is underemployment. We accomplish less than we could. But it is the disengaged mind that has the liberty to see alternatives—to hear the whispers to which a harried and hurried world is insensitive. Leaving our conscious mind somewhat vacant is an invitation for matter hitherto hidden in unconsciousness to assert its presence. Most thinkers and writers have experience of revelations and solutions coming at the most unlikely moment. Whether we are in the bath, almost asleep, pausing at the corner of the stairs, or just goofing off, suddenly the clouds may part and the sun shines through. The novelist Don De Lillo describes the process in this way:

> A writer takes earnest measures to secure his solitude and then finds endless ways to squander it. . . . One's personality and vision are shaped by other writers, by movies, by paintings, by music. But the work itself, you know—sentence by sentence, page by page—it's much too intimate, much too private, to come from anywhere but deep within the writer himself. It comes out of all the time a writer wastes. We stand around, look out the window, walk down the hall, come back to the page, and, in those intervals, something subterranean is forming, a literal dream that comes out of day-dreaming. It's too deep to be attributed to clear sources.[21]

Our best accomplishments derive from all the time we have wasted. What an idea! How odd this sentiment seems to those who embrace a work ethic. What it is saying is that our most creative moments come when we are responsive to the promptings of the unspeaking universe. The true artist is one who gives hand, heart, or tongue to the service of a tradition that has been received and assimilated, and now finds sparkling expression in something never seen or heard before. In the work of creation, the tradition comes alive. For this to happen the artist must have learned how to be silent, to become a disciple, to be formed. Without this only a degenerate self-expression results that is of interest to no one.

We were made to be creative, and if this natural propensity is blocked, whether by overwork or by idleness, we become irritable disturbers of the peace in whatever community we live and work. As we have already noted, the key to understanding leisure is to see it as a means of giving a high priority to the present moment. We have to seize the opportunities that this day offers. Beyond the external discipline that keeps us constant in the performance of our task, a certain mental vigilance is required. This means that we do not allow ourselves to be dominated and determined by thoughts and feelings from the past; we have to cast off these shackles. Nor can we reduce present opportunities to wishful thinking about the future. Daydreaming can never be a substitute for action. We are all familiar with stories of those who have become reconciled with a terminal disease that leaves them but a short time to live. They make up their minds to live every day to the full—not to postpone the good that is today within their reach, not to fail to exploit the potential richness of every hour. What a blessing if we could live in like manner.

There are two happy outcomes to a satisfactory resolution of the issue of leisure: mindfulness and patience. Mindfulness comes from having learned to listen to reality and not reducing it to echoes of what is happening inside ourselves. We put aside our heedless habits and begin to pay serious attention to the world outside. Today matters. This is the day the Lord has made; it is the only one that we have. From this we have also come to realize that before we act, we need to accept that there is a season for everything under the sun (Eccl. 3:1). Leisure teaches us to recognize that everything is to be done at the opportune time, as

Benedict insists (31:18, 68:2). We have learned to read the signs of the times as a means of ensuring that our action is called forth by the objective needs of the situation and not by our own subjective need to act. In many cases we need space and time to consider at what moment our contribution will bear the fairest fruit. In the final analysis, leisure is a school of wisdom.

4 | *Reading*

They are free for reading.
RB 48:4

The silent attentiveness of true leisure enables us to find meaning in our lives. We need space to step back from issues to assess their significance more surely. There is an apt saying of Seneca to the effect that leisure without reading is meaningless. The two activities go hand in hand. That is why Benedict uses the expression *vacare lectioni*. Reading, especially *lectio divina*, is not to be reduced to a task that somehow must be fitted in alongside other necessary occupations. To read well one must be at leisure. Disinterested reading involves moving into a different zone that permits placid reflection. A good book, like good wine, cannot be savored in hurry. It needs room to breathe. A mind cluttered with many preoccupations is not free for reading, nor is a body that cannot sit still and let the world go by without it.

1. Escape from Meaning

Creating an empty space is one of the most daunting challenges we face. Nature abhors a vacuum. There are always many activities and non-activities that clamor for our attention, seeping into a disengaged mind and quickly filling it. We can have some sympathy, I suppose, when the invaders represent real necessities or positive advantages to others. More often than not, however, it will be a case of tasks multiplying to consume whatever time is available, manufactured urgencies that present themselves only when we attempt to be still.

The value of reading is best demonstrated by noting the ill effects of its absence in the lives of those who give themselves to idleness and fantasy, *qui vacat otio aut fabulis* (48:18, 43:8). Because the structure of monastic life provides time and opportunity for interior pursuits, it follows that those who have little inclination for these must find other means of filling in the day. If it is true that acedia is a dominant characteristic of contemporary Western societies,[22] then the most obvious symptom of this malaise must be a flight from boredom and the relentless search for excitement and entertainment.

Bernard of Clairvaux was of the opinion that in every monastery can be found the four kinds of monks described by St. Benedict in his first chapter. The wandering about which is not good for their souls (66:7) can easily take place without moving outside the enclosure.

> Then there are carnal gyrovagues. Only their bodies are enclosed within the walls of the monastery. Their hearts and their tongues circulate throughout the whole world.[23]

This happened in the twelfth century. It happens more easily today since the expectations about what constitutes "the good life" that new recruits bring with them to the monastery are not always sufficiently challenged. To many, a low-impact environment seems a very dim mode of existence.

What is the dominant mode of experience at the end of the twentieth century? How do people see things, and how do they expect to see things? The answer is simple. In every field, from business to politics to marketing to education, the dominant mode has become entertainment. . . . In other centuries human beings wanted to be saved, or improved, or freed, or educated. But in our century, they want to be entertained. The great fear is not of disease or death, but of boredom.[24]

The causes behind this insistence on being amused are grave. Behind the happy faces are empty heads and hearts. Entertainment becomes necessary when life has lost all meaning—where nothing in the outside world connects with or energizes what is going on within. So some insulation against the jarring effects of reality becomes necessary. When I was young, dentists discovered the utility of having tropical fish in the surgery to distract the active imaginations of children from conjuring up nameless horrors about to be inflicted on them. In the same way we escape into the world of virtual happiness and canned laughter to avoid confronting the possibility that the real world may make demands on us.

The nihilistic culture propagated by so many countries in the West emphasizes neutrality among options. We are free to choose whatever suits us best—something becomes right by the fact of our choosing it. No particular option has any greater right to be chosen than any other. This denial of the objectivity of values leads to economic rationalism, consumerism, the unbridled pursuit of wealth and power, substance abuse, sexual permissiveness, the relativity of commitments, family break-ups, disregard for the rights of others and especially of the powerless, the abuse of children, abortion, euthanasia, wars of opportunity, and generally what in 1995 Pope John Paul II termed "the culture of death." It does not take much acumen to conclude that a consumer society is well on the way to becoming a consumptive society.

> The culture of death is simultaneously a culture dominated by the notion of "entertainment." . . . The very notion of entertainment presumes the state of boredom as the norm, which means that a culture increasingly fueled by this notion assumes that our lives are innately and intrinsically meaningless without the constant stream of "stimulation" and distraction, a stream inevitably subject to the law of diminishing returns.[25]

Maybe some will say that the mass media are more froth and bubble than toil and trouble. This may be true if we do not look to the cumulative effect of daily exposure. What happens is like the spam that bedevils e-mail; it is fatuous and not persuasive, but it clogs up the channels of communication. I have no doubt of the degenerative effect on the mind that results from sustained exposure to the mass media, where images sometimes swamp critical thought, where opinion is proposed as knowledge, where sincerity is more highly regarded than truth,[26] and where anything can be "spun" to mean whatever the commentator chooses.

In the lives of many of our contemporaries, television and the Internet play a constructive role or contribute substantially to their contentment. The fact that there are many benefits in information technology does not necessarily mean that those who accept the guidance of the Rule of Benedict can accept modern means of social communication unquestioningly. Just because they exist does not automatically mean that they will have a positive effect in the pursuit of the Benedictine ideal. Both the content and the extent of exposure need to be monitored and assayed. Having different goals means choosing distinctive means.

Reading is a cool medium that invites us to step back and ponder critically what we have encountered. We can stop at any time and compare what we read from what we know from other sources. We can build bridges between the text and our own experience and so achieve some measure of fusion of horizons. Solid reading trains us to think issues through for ourselves. Television, on the other hand, is a hot medium: It speaks directly to the emotions and more often than not passes on subliminal messages through camera angles, graphic images, editing, and even deliberate falsification. Its easy accessibility means that we often approach it in an uncritical state of mind, allowing ourselves to be formed by what we see, believing that we are experiencing the world immediately and as it is, instead of absorbing the particular bias that program makers wish to communicate. Television is food for the mind that is meant to be swallowed without being chewed.

> TV favors a mentality in which certain things no longer matter particularly: skills like the ability to enjoy a complex argument, for instance, or to perceive nuances, or to keep in mind large amounts of significant information, or to remember today what someone said last month, or to consider strong and carefully argued opinions in defiance of what is conventionally called "balance." Its content lurches between violence of action, emotional hyperbole and blandness of opinion. And it never, never stops. It is always trying to give us something interesting. Not interesting for long: just for now. Commercial TV teaches people to scorn complexity and to feel, not to think. It has come to present society as a pagan circus of freaks, pseudo-heroes and wild morons struggling on the sands of a Colosseum without walls. . . .[27]

Thomas Merton was adamant that television—at least American television—was a danger for any who are interested in progressing further in the practice of contemplation. He expresses himself on the subject with characteristic verve, a little acerbity, and a not-untypical degree of exaggeration.

> The life of a television-watcher is a kind of caricature of contemplation. Passivity, uncritical absorption, receptivity, inertia. Not only that, but a gradual yielding to the mystic attraction until one is spellbound in a state of complete union. The trouble with this caricature is that it is really the exact opposite of contemplation: for true contemplation is precisely the fruit of a most active and intransigent rupture with all that captivates the senses, the emotions, and the will on a material or temporal level. The contemplative reaches his passivity only after terrific struggle with everything that appeals to his appetites as a half-animal member of the human herd. He is receptive and still only because the stillness he has reached is lucid, spiritual, and full of liberty. It is the summit of a life of spiritual freedom. The other, the ersatz, is the nadir of intellectual and emotional slavery.[28]

The danger of servitude, especially to the electronic media, is not only that it wastes time and incapacitates, but it also serves as a channel through which the evil thoughts about which Benedict speaks (*cogitationes malas*, 4:50), enter the mind of the monk or nun and thence pass through to the community. I am not speaking merely about lubricious thoughts—the "scurrilities" to which Benedict was so uncompromisingly opposed—I am thinking of the erosion of fundamental values and the coarsening of the mind itself that result from daily preoccupation with triviality. When the beliefs and values weaken, only external constraint holds us to monastic praxis, and the level of *joie de vivre* ineluctably declines.

At the end of a day's work, many people prefer the easy passivity of watching television to the alert perusal of the printed page, and that is understandable. At the same time, those who express a desire for wisdom and wish to grow in spirituality are often surprised at the suggestion that they unplug the television. Few people are honest enough to admit to the hours spent watching and half-watching television. If they kept records and devoted half the hours so consumed to silence, reading, reflection, meditation, and serious conversation, I think they would begin to notice a considerable difference in the quality of their lives.

2. In a Nook with a Book

The situation for those who have chosen to be followers of Benedict is somewhat different. Part of their vocation, it seems to me, is to be lovers of the book.[29] Someone absorbed in reading is a beautiful sight, as many great paintings attest. Observing, we become aware of a certain stillness of body and quietness of mind in the reader, a concentration of energies and a healing withdrawal from the anguish of life. It is a moment of ecstasy: a retreat from direct involvement with one part of reality in order to be re-energized by contact with reality's less visible component. The act of reading symbolizes something of what monastic life is all about: withdrawal from what is apparent to seek the reality that underlies appearances, in solitude, in silence, in recollection.

Undoubtedly Benedict sees reading as a means of keeping a monk out of mischief when he has nothing else to do, but there is more to it than that. Reading is at the service of a reflective life; it contributes greatly to the gravitas that Benedict prized. Not only does it broaden the mind by extending the range of interests, but it also brings about a certain refinement that is the opposite of coarseness or vulgarity. If we believe that growth in spirituality coincides with a more complete fulfillment of human potential, then we will not be surprised at the proposition that a good monk is a fully alive human being. The leisure that ideally is an essential component of everyday monastic life offers to monks and nuns the opportunity to become more profound people—not just more knowledgeable, not walking, talking encyclopedias, but persons who have integrated what they have learned into the fabric of their life.

In fact, monastic poverty ensures that nowadays monastic libraries are small and eclectic compared with the vast and systematic collections in universities. It is not the quantity of books read that is important but the zeal for truth and wisdom embodied in the act of reading.

> What is the use of innumerable books and librar-
> ies if the owner is unable to read them all in a
> lifetime? A student will be burdened by a crowd
> of authors, not instructed. It is much better to
> devote yourself to a few authors than to lose
> your way among a multitude.[30]

In the same way, the idea that speed-reading is the sign of an educated person defeats the purpose of the sort of reading most suitable for monasteries. Monastic reading is not exclusively intended for the extraction of information in the most efficient and expeditious manner. A monk reads two books simultaneously, the text as it lies open before him and a more inner source of enlightenment that the medievals termed "the book of experience." What is written on the page is read in parallel with the lessons learned through living. Reflection on experience helps readers to understand what the text is saying, and understanding the text helps the reader to unravel the complexities of experience. As

St. Athanasius wrote, "The Psalms are, for those who recite them, a sort of mirror in which they can view the movements of their own soul."[31] Reading well practiced is a way to the heart.

Delight and enlightenment from reading depend on our paying close attention. Rushing through a book to reach its finish will, more often than not, yield little fruit. Rapid reading delivers to us the most superficial layer of the text's meaning; to find its deeper sense we often have to read the text several times, stopping to mull over the meaning of words and phrases, and stepping back to survey the logical development of the theme as a whole. This is how Allen Bloom describes close reading in a well-expressed paragraph that I have often quoted.

> A line-by-line, word-by-word analysis must be undertaken. . . . The hardest thing of all is the simplest to formulate: every word must be understood. It is hard because the eye tends to skip over just those things which are the most shocking or most call into question our way of looking at things. . . . The argument or example that seems irrelevant, trivial or boring is precisely the one most likely to be a sign of what is outside one's framework and which it calls into question. One passes over such things unless one takes pencil and paper, outlines, counts, stops at everything and tries to wonder.[32]

Our reading is meant to take us somewhere, not merely to leave us where we are, to ease our doubts and reinforce our prejudices. A good book is an invitation to grow beyond what we are at present, to view issues from a different perspective, to add new elements to our personal synthesis. We must not allow our innate resistance to change or render this process impotent. Reading is dialogical: We are not asked to sell out on our most cherished beliefs and values the moment we find them contradicted, but there is no harm in engaging in a conversation that will enable us to nuance our position in response to implied or explicit criticism. Trying to understand a mentality that is foreign to us often serves as a means of bringing to the surface of consciousness deeply held convictions that hitherto we have not closely examined or explored.

For every Christian, and especially for the monk, reading is important in order to shore up the distinctive structure of beliefs and values that is necessary if we are to live a life worthy of the gospel and to be strangers to the ways of the world. The more exposure we have to unevangelical modes of thinking or systems of values, the more we have to keep reminding ourselves that we have freely chosen a different path. "Reading is an essential part of the *ascesis* that leads from the visible to the invisible, or from the sign to what is signified."[33] We are also obliged to equip ourselves to explain to others the faith by which we live. "Always be ready to offer an apologia for the hope that is in you to anyone who asks you for an explanation" (1 Pet. 3:15). As we keep insisting, actions are not enough; they need to be sustained by appropriate beliefs and values. Otherwise motivation will melt away and we will cease our effort to lead a good life.

A final aspect of general reading is probably more important than it seems at first glance. If we acquire good habits of reading then it begins to be a source of enjoyment and refreshment that helps us to recuperate from more taxing occupations. Moreover, a good book can be a welcome friend during hard times. Reading is not expensive, it can be done almost anywhere, and it does not require the participation of others. It often creates a helpful distance between us and the source of our anxieties, not allowing our troubles to keep invading consciousness, but indirectly permitting to acquire a better perspective on things. It lets

our minds rest while a response is being generated in the
unconscious.

3. *Lectio Divina*

For anyone thoroughly committed to Christian and
monastic ideals it soon becomes apparent that these ideals
quickly lose definition if they are not constantly re-applied to
each changing situation. Without attention and application,
our beliefs and values become fuzzy and begin to blend with
philosophies in which the distinctiveness of the gospel is not
primary. All reading is good, and useful in coming to a
personal stance before reality. Best of all, however, is that
reading that allows us to keep deepening our grasp on our
central convictions and commitments. This means that some
species of "spiritual reading" is important for all who want
to remain faithful to their baptismal promise to live by the
Spirit and not according to the flesh. It must be something to
keep the flame of faith burning bright.

In this regard what works for one need not be as effective
for all. Our situations are different. In a general way we all
need to be brought into an ever-deeper relationship with
Christ, to be instructed by his teaching, to be inspired to
imitate his example, and to grow in a sense of friendship
and personal loyalty. We all need to keep applying the
content of our religious beliefs to the concrete circumstances
of our life, to ensure that the obedience of faith is a lived
reality. We all need to stir up our hope in the future promised
by God, to keep alive our spiritual desire and to prevent our
being overcome by the cares and anxieties of today. And we
all need to be drawn to an ever-warmer and more intense
prayer that goes beyond religious formalism and really
enables us to come humbly into the presence of God.

How these goals are realized will depend on many subjective
factors: our education, the opportunities and resources

available to us, and even our mental, emotional, and physical well-being. Whatever our present circumstances, however, we cannot afford to ignore God's self-revelation, because in it are contained the challenges that will guide our choices and the comfort that will sustain them. Cut off from God's Word, our lives are adrift. This is not to say that everyone has to curl up in a corner with a Greek New Testament—desirable though that may be. But all of us need to ensure that God's Word has access to our lives, whether by reading the Scriptures directly or at one or several removes, by hearing them read, by having their meaning mediated by fellow-believers, or in some other way. We need to feed our minds on the gospel message, to ponder it in our hearts and to become, in our own small way, doers of God's Word.

In monastic circles during the last fifty years there has been a renewed interest in the exercise of *lectio divina*. Whether such reading, as it is now practiced, exactly corresponds to what happened in ancient and medieval monasteries is unimportant. The point is that it is almost impossible to envisage perseverance in lifelong commitment without the regular dedication of periods of time to the reading of the Scriptures and other texts that feed our faith. Indissolubly associated with this reading are reflection and obedient application, prayer and contemplation. Most monks and nuns feel that the liturgy and other communal readings are not enough to sustain them. They experience the call to add to the common commitment, some personal dedication of time and energy so that they can wait upon the Lord in expectant silence. This is necessarily an individual exercise, tailored to suit personal possibilities and particular vocations, but it also builds community. "What ascends must converge." The more a person's consciousness and behavior are submitted to ongoing evangelization, the more harmonious is the interface with other people. Those who do not regularly expose their thoughts and actions to the judgment of the revealed word are more likely to poison their relationships with others because of their own inconsistencies.

This is not the place to reproduce all that I have written elsewhere about *lectio divina*.[34] I would simply like to emphasize the idea that the most important difference between sacred reading and other reading is the fact that *lectio* is a work of love, a gift of self through the dedication of time. It is not looking for self-enhancement, but simply to enter more consciously into a sense of the presence of God, in reverence and submission, ready to be instructed, corrected, or consoled as it pleases God. For the moment, it is a yielding of our lives into the control of Another. And if it sometimes seems that the time spent is more like prayer than reading, so be it. At the same time good habits of general reading such as the ability to sit still for a while, the skill of close reading, and the taste for pondering, will certainly provide a good foundation on which the lifetime practice of *lectio divina* may be built.

Lectio divina is an integral part of the Benedictine way of life, especially in our days when most people are literate and in need of some antidote to the toxic effects of ambient culture. Because of their greater need for distance, monks and nuns are in greater need for counter-balancing reading. Our very particular vocation demands not only an increased dedication of time, but it also expects a certain distinctiveness in what we draw from our reading. That this was recognized even in the twelfth century is clear from an exhortation that Aelred of Rievaulx addressed to his monks.

> But you, my friends, have renounced the works of this world and so that you are now released from every worldly care and anxiety and give yourselves to warfare with unclean spirits and your own thoughts. Therefore there is a different reason for meditating on the Scriptures, a different necessity.[35]

Monastic *lectio* operates within the context of a relatively innocent life and a high degree of self-scrutiny. The Scriptures are the key to a delicate sensitivity to the nuances of good and evil in very minor situations. Such delicacy asks for keenness in listening and promptness in obeying even in small matters. For this to be possible, close attention is necessary both to the obvious meaning of what is read and to what is hidden beneath the surface. Such micro-reading is an art that must be learned through a period of apprenticeship as a necessary part of mindful living and faithful discipleship.

5 | *Chastity*

To love chastity
RB 4:64

Saint Benedict's call to "love chastity" is another strong indication that he wants us to live at a distance from the ways of the world. Few modern societies, particularly in the West, take chastity seriously or believe that unchastity renders a person less honorable. Much of our literary and theatrical culture condones sexual immorality in a way that would cause massive offense if the sins concerned offenses against popular virtues. To defend chastity publicly seems like fanaticism, and even its practice is regarded by many as eccentric and even unhealthy. Youth movements that advocate postponement of sexual activity until marriage are scornfully reported by the mass media. Those who suggest that promiscuity might be a factor in the spread of AIDS or other sexually transmitted diseases are howled down. Serial divorces and their sorry residues are accepted as a normal part of modern life. Fidelity seems as outdated as medieval chivalry.

It is probably true that no other area of morality spawns so great a suspicion of hypocrisy as sexual behavior. Because sexuality is a private area in which secrecy is appropriate, there is a general assumption that much more is going on than we hear about. Beyond this, it is certainly true that in the sexual morality of most of us there is considerable area of ambiguity, due not only to weakness of will, but also to the fact that nature, through the agency of the sexual instinct and the habits and imaginations associated with it, is persistently recalcitrant, refusing to operate within the parameters of personal choice. The persistence and independence of sexual tendencies is an embarrassment to most of us. Because they are conscious of their own failings and because they fear that advocacy might be considered as a cloak for a double life, many are reluctant to promote chastity. The less its praises are sung, the less likelihood there is that chastity will gain many followers.

Priestly celibacy and monastic chastity that involve the renunciation of all direct sexual activity are scarcely believable in many cultures. This is why it becomes necessary to build up a fund of beliefs and values that support chastity. It is not enough to talk about behavior alone, we need to think in terms of motivation. "Just say 'No!'" is a beguilingly simple recommendation, but it fails to address more fundamental issues. Celibate chastity is possible as a lifelong commitment only when, by God's grace, a person is animated by an ardent spiritual desire—this is what ancient monks referred to as "fighting fire with fire." The eunuchs Jesus praised were those who became so for the sake of the kingdom.

1. Understanding Chastity

It is not enough to preach chastity, be we ever so eloquent. In the early years of monastic experience, a solid and detailed factual knowledge is needed together with a re-formation of conscience. Otherwise newcomers may find themselves stranded in mid-life without a solid and fully internalized value system. This proactive task of formation is more challenging than simple accompaniment. Resistance may be encountered. Re-framing one's personal philosophy is even more demanding than changing a lifestyle. Chastity is a task: We do not enter monastic life because we are chaste, but in order to become chaste. This means developing the skills that will help us toward that goal. These include a good understanding of sexuality, the capacity to share with a mentor, skills of self-acceptance and self-appreciation, skills of intimacy within appropriate boundaries, and skills of autonomy—accepting responsibility for the choices that we make and for their consistency with our fundamental vocational option. Such a program is not going to be accomplished overnight. It will certainly take time, it will probably need the guidance and support of another, and it will be punctuated by periods of difficulty, temptation, and at least partial failure. It has long been the conviction of those much exercised in this virtue that progress is possible only when we begin to rely on God's grace and not on our own merits or achievements.

At the level of doctrine it becomes necessary to impart a body of teaching that approaches chastity practically, inclusively, and attractively. Practically, in that it does not avoid any of the physiological, psychological, or behavioral aspects associated with sexuality, but presents them in a way that is accurate, clear, and unthreatening. Inclusively, so that it respects the diversity of sexual experience and honors the particular journey that each has to make to arrive at chastity. Attractively, in that it presents chastity as one pathway to human fulfillment, as a condition and means of satisfying the deep desire for spiritual experience. Chastity is also a "way that leads to life" (Prol. 20).

The bottom line of monastic chastity remains **self-restraint**. In this the discipline of monastic life can be a help. Those who have become practised in recognizing and reading the thoughts that lead to gluttony, anger, and sloth are familiar with the necessity of not allowing the promptings of nature to go unchecked. Likewise, with experience, we begin to recognize the particular situations in which sexual temptation awaits a slackening of vigilance, and we can take measures to avoid them or otherwise to protect ourselves. Often enough the resistance we are called to offer is humdrum and routine. An inner voice may whisper, "Why bother?" but we will soon learn that sexual arousal is more easily reversed in its beginnings than after momentum has built. Those who have been brainwashed to regard renunciation as unworthy will have a hard time with monastic chastity. It is foolish to think otherwise. The system of asceticism that is an integral element in the Benedictine way of life is incomplete without a practical commitment to chastity.

There is always a danger that the theory and practice of chastity can become an accomplice of sexual repression. The particular disaster that this brings about is not so much unchastity as a miserable existence. Monks and nuns may go through life unnecessarily burdened by sexual guilt and shame, fearful to confront the real issues and secretly believing themselves worse than the rest. Or a secret life may develop, split off from the beliefs and values that shape an otherwise worthy monastic career. This is why genuine chastity, distinct from mere sexual abstinence, is built on **truthfulness**—accepting one's sexuality fully and attempting to integrate it into the whole fabric of personal, Christian, and monastic existence.

The truth of chastity calls us to a fully conscious acceptance and appreciation of the role of sexuality in our lives. It is one of the surest signs of growth in humility. It is not, however, a gloomy admission of guilt, but a happy and clear-sighted acceptance of what we are by nature, who we are by personal choice, and what we might become when the grace of God works its way with us. Truth obliges me to be able to make the following assertions:

- I am a human being; my personal history includes moments of weakness, blindness, and malice. There are numerous incidents in my past and present that appropriately cause me to feel ashamed or guilty.
- As a being that is both bodily and spiritual, I experience within myself contrary impulses; I am tempted. In me also, "the flesh lusts against the spirit."
- At the level of thought, desire, and action my practice of chastity has been imperfect.
- I am an adult male/female and I admit that my sexual instincts are often independent of and contrary to my self-definition and my personal choices.
- I accept my personal sexual history as a sign of God's providence in my regard.
- I recognize my sexual orientation and accept it.
- I have sexual needs and desires.
- Sexual attraction influences what I do and the choices I make.
- I believe that sexual restraint is possible with God's grace.
- I accept the consequences of my conversion and vocation with its commitment to celibate chastity.
- I believe that our human needs for relationship, intimacy, and love can be satisfied within the context of celibate fidelity.

One who has come to the point of being able to keep such truths in mind will probably find that the practice of chastity simply fits into the fabric of monastic life, drawing its energy from its various components, particularly the habitual discipline, the life in community, and the constant return to God in prayer. There may be periods of crisis in chastity, just as there may be hard times with regard to obedience or stability. But if the rest of monastic observance is sound the trouble will pass and its only effects will be positive.

We need to speak more about the advantages of chastity. From the ancient monastic masters we can learn also about the **freedom** that genuine chastity heralds—freedom from unhealthy psychological tendencies and mechanisms and the tyranny of sub-personal forces—the passions and vices, the control exercised by bad habits, the conditioning by our past experience and social context, and our narcissistic tendencies to exploit others. Freedom to live the monastic life without compromise, to love others without jeopardizing our commitment to celibacy, and to move more deeply and fully into contemplative experience.

There is much in monastic tradition that can facilitate this task, particularly in the writings of John Cassian.

> For Cassian chastity was the defining virtue of the perfect monk. It was the ground of contemplative insight, ecstatic prayer and spiritual knowledge. Only the perfection of chastity, he claimed, can lead to the heights of love, and only from there can we hope to ascend to the image and likeness of God that is one's birthright.[36]

With such a lofty goal, it becomes evident that genuine chastity cannot be simply the result of human effort. It is the sphere par excellence in which we experience the regenerating and all-embracing power of divine grace. Our imperfect chastity leads us to prayer; dogged prayer brings with it an experience of healing, and as our hearts become less conflicted, they become more transparent to the ever-present reality of God.

Chastity is a quality or virtue that results from the interaction of self-restraint, truthfulness, and emerging freedom. Turning things inside out, we could say that unchastity is the lack of self-restraint—it is the result of an uncontrolled, disordered, intemperate life. It is untruthful because it denies our call to virtue. It habitually gives birth to non-transparency and dishonesty. It is often unfree, because our inconsistent behavior is more often than not compulsive and out of harmony with the direction we want our lives to assume.

2. A Spirituality of Chastity

Experience reveals that chastity is a complex virtue. Mere sexual abstinence does not begin to exhaust its possibilities and will probably not endure unless it is supported by a whole range of contributory beliefs and values. In the lives of different monks and nuns the relative proportion of the elements varies, but, for most, chastity will be a realistic prospect to the extent that their lives are characterized by the following qualities:

a) A Discerning Sense of Responsibility

As adults we are morally responsible only for the choices that we make and for the situations into which we get ourselves. At the level of feeling we do not always distinguish between shame (or even disgust) and guilt; we feel equally bad about aspects of our sexuality that are natural and involuntary and those that are the result of choice. There is so much denial in the area of sexuality—particularly among religious people—that avoidance often makes us unaware of the exact location of the frontier between free activity and happenstance. When many issues of sexuality are resolutely unrecognized and undiscussed they become fuzzy, and our attempts to practise a sane chastity become less well motivated. Some clarity of self-vision is necessary so that the sexual restraint to which we have committed ourselves becomes a feature of daily living. We are talking about a well-formed conscience. Conscience has two roles, one to throw light on potential courses of action, the other to pass judgment on what has been already done. In both its legislative and judicial functions, conscience needs to be ruled by reason. It needs, as we have said previously, diligently to search out the truth. Conscience is not merely an enforcer of maximalist morality.

A good conscience is marked by a high degree of discernment. It does not accept moral responsibility for realities outside the direct control of the will. In sexual matters, as we all know, our capacity to be aroused belongs to our nature—to *what* we are. It is often not the result of choice. Mostly we do not choose our sexual orientation, the specificities of our sexual sensibility to arousal, and many elements of our personal history that have generated our particular needs. This means that the early stages of sexual excitement can be pre-voluntary—and are, in fact, often unwelcome. Habit, likewise, is a "second nature"; it can often push particular actions outside the realm of fully free choice and diminish our liability. A maximalist conscience can burden us with an unreasonable degree of inhibition and guilt. The result of this is not only unhappiness but a moral confusion that can lead to scrupulosity and desperation on the one hand, or indifference and a kind of fatalism on the other. We are responsible for our actions, certainly, but there is no need to feel guilty where no freedom existed, just as it is dishonorable to evade responsibility for choices that were either the immediate or remote sources of temptation.

b) Ownership of Weakness

Part of the advantage of trying to be chaste is that we very soon discover that it is impossible to succeed in any meaningful way by our own efforts. In the unlikely event that there was an annual prize of millions of dollars for the most chaste person in the world, I wonder how many would submit their names. Most of us feel that our hold on this virtue is tenuous, at best, and liable to be temporary. We feel fragile enough, if not in behavior, then certainly in feeling and thought. Even advancing age is no certain bulwark. Considering the past and the present, we are all somewhat imperfect in our practice of chastity, to say the least. And there are no guarantees about the future.

The healthiest way of handling this weakness is to accept it as a reality and then to take care to incorporate it into our basic philosophy of life. Another way of saying this is that humility and chastity go hand in hand. This is certainly the view of St. Aelred.

> Everyone who desires to be freed from the domination of fleshly passions should exert themselves with great zeal and labor to acquire or preserve humility. The whole perfection of chastity and inner quiet consists in the perfection of humility.[37]

> Whoever loses humility is not able to keep chastity of the flesh . . . because when the soul is polluted by pride, the flesh is also polluted by sexual sin.[38]

Our achievement-oriented culture does not much like weakness or imperfection, and so we find it hard not to sweep our limitations out of awareness so that neither we nor others ever refer to them. How stupid can you get? When I know I have an allergy, I take steps to reduce my contact with whatever it is to which I am allergic. If I have a physical or mental liability, I re-route operations so that I do not have to rely on something that will likely let me down. If I am afraid of heights I don't get a job as a steeplejack. If I can't add, I invest in a calculator. You don't have to be Einstein to understand the principle. When I recognize that the lifelong commitment to sexual restraint is going to be a bit tricky in my case, then I set about finding ways to prevent an unnecessary disaster.[39] In the last analysis, this involves reinforcing my sense of dependence on God. If it takes a mess to make that happen, so be it. But there are more immediate things I can do to ease matters.

My ownership of weakness will probably never be complete unless I take the step of declaring it in the presence of another person. I am not thinking here so much of the anonymity of sacramental confession, as of the more open disclosure of my fragility to another equally fragile human being. Trusting another sufficiently to reveal my secret will make it more difficult for me afterwards to deny it or re-interpret the evidence in a more favorable light.

c) Acceptance of Discipline

Have I got to the point of saying, "I don't know about everybody else, but I have to be a bit careful in the area of sexuality"? If so, I am probably ready to recognize the need for a discipline of life that will enable me to move towards the ultimate goal of my life. As a follower of Benedict I have come to the monastery seeking God: I need to be serious about countering anything that gets in the way of that primary purpose. Disordered sexuality is not going to help me on my way. This means, as we have already noted, admitting the necessity of asceticism in our lives as a general principle. It is not only a matter of trying to be careful about specifically sexual occasions of sin; common sense dictates that we attack the roots of sin as well as its branches.[40] "For as long as we are tempted by carnal delights, it is necessary for us to tame the flesh of the body by vigils, fasts, and labor."[41] Chastity is impossible without some supporting bodily observances. The means that we use indicate that we are aware of the need for vigilance, the ability to refrain from or refuse the satisfaction of bodily appetites, and the necessity of being proactive in implementing whatever measures seem necessary. Along with at least a symbolic degree of bodily mortification, there is need for vigilance and care regarding our thoughts. Again, Aelred has something to say about this.

> Our flock is made up of our good feelings and our good thoughts. Over these flocks it is necessary for us to be vigilant, lest our enemy prevail over us and take them away from us, scattering and dispersing them. They are vigilant over their flock who carefully guard all their thoughts, words and works lest in some way they are led into falling. The same is true of those who keep guard over their senses.[42]

Chastity does not just happen; especially for us who have vowed it, it is a task to be done. "If you really want to be celibate, celibacy must be among the most important elements in your life."[43] This means that in response to God's grace we need to spend time, use energy, and employ both intellect and will in making it happen.

d) Patience

We are not going to become chaste overnight. That is not God's plan. The spiritual warfare that is involved in avoiding defeat at the hands of unchastity is near enough to lifelong. It is the labor of wrestling with unchastity that gradually makes us chaste, growing in experience of the enemy's tactics, motivated by the pain of our wounds to avoid exposing ourselves needlessly to attack, building up confidence in the resources that are available, and, above all, learning to trust in the promise, "My grace is sufficient for you" (2 Cor. 12:9).

Sexual temptation can come from within ourselves or from outside. Sometimes it seems to come from nowhere. Temptation tempers the spirit. Without it virtue is slack because it has not yet learned where the boundaries between good and evil are located, how to restrain itself from heedlessly crossing those boundaries, and how to be strong when confronted with the urgency of contrary attractions.

> Patience is the greatest of all the virtues. . . . It can be divided into two parts: temperance and fortitude, since it possesses the soul both in prosperity and in adversity. It makes it sober and strong against the filthy pruritus of the flesh and the surging of interior vices, as also against the exterior enticements and cruelties of the world.[44]

There is a lot of virtue involved in accepting the slowness of the process of becoming chaste, living with patent imperfection, and feeling pain at the distance between cherished ideals and actual performance. The discontent generated by our temptations and infidelities is probably the most effective teacher of chastity. More often than not our compromises are due more to the wobbliness of our will and the strength of our instincts than to any fully free personal choice. As St. Augustine notes, "Often sins occur because of ignorance or human weakness, and, in fact, many are committed by people weeping and groaning in distress." As a result the precariousness of the virtue of chastity is more of a burden than a sin. It is a constant reminder of the uncertainty of our perseverance in the life to which we have been called and an effective incentive to prayer for help. Especially, since many people in monastic life are natural high-achievers, their lack of tangible progress in this area serves as a good reminder that not everything depends on talent and energy. Some things come only by way of gift.

e) Hope

Patience is animated by the theological virtue of hope. "We know that troubles bring about patience, and patience serves as a means of probation which leads to hope" (Rom. 5:3-4). There is an eschatological character about all Christian virtue, but especially chastity. No other virtue is so other-worldly, having little recompense in the here and now. That is probably why Jesus speaks of those who have committed themselves fully to the kingdom as eunuchs (Mt. 19:12). Despite the promise of the hundredfold, they receive few collateral benefits in this life for the sacrifice they have made; their hope is for the future.

Chastity makes no sense at all except on the basis of faith in the promise of eternal life and on the validity of our call to monasticism as a way to that life. The *Suscipe* sung at the moment of solemn profession can serve as a lifelong motif for prayer with special reference to chastity: "Sustain me, O Christ, according to your promise and I shall live; do not disappoint me of my hope" (58:21). How many people support their efforts to reduce their appetite for food by jumping on the scales to check out their weight loss! Each success motivates them to continue with the program. There is nothing comparable with chastity. We can't measure our progress, nor can we afford to be too pleased with ourselves. And, in our culture, we find it hard to persevere in a discipline that does not yield tangible results or any prospect of immediate gratification. Something extraordinary is required.

As we shall see later, chastity cannot exist in an affective void. The hope that makes chastity practicable is not just a matter of waiting without any evidence that the situation will improve. It is much more like eager anticipation of something that is certain—like the end of winter and the burgeoning of better days. Monastic life is based entirely on faith; if there is no future life it loses its specific meaning. "If for this life only we have hope in Christ Jesus, then of all people are we the most to be pitied" (1 Cor. 15:19). Our efforts to become chaste are one means of putting into practice the otherwise disembodied virtues of faith and hope—and they can become a very sincere expression of the love that binds us to God and to other people. It is not for our own benefit that we practise sexual restraint: It is because the kingdom of God is active within us, and it is for the sake of the kingdom that we accept to struggle with the task.

There is a certain sense in which the experience of chastity is one of being *suspended* between heaven and earth, having separated ourselves from the pleasures of earth but not yet having attained to the joys of heaven.[45] In another sense, as Bernard insists in his teaching on Advent, we are occasionally fortified for the onward journey by anticipatory experience of the spiritual world. There is some continuity between Christian experience now and what may be expected in the hereafter. And so, it has to be said that it is through prayer that chastity becomes feasible. Conversely it is because of ongoing struggle with unchastity that many are led to prayer, according to Augustine's maxim: "Because we are human we are not strong. Because we are not strong we pray."[46]

The psychologist Richard Sipe, who has done more than most to expose the fragility of religious celibacy, sees prayer as an essential component in its practice. "It is the connection with the Ultimate Other that undergirds, infuses and crowns the celibate quest."[47]

> In studying religious celibacy for thirty-five years I have never found one exception to this fundamental rule: Prayer is necessary to maintain the celibate process. A neglectful prayer life ensures failure of celibate integration. . . . No matter at what point in or out of the celibate

process you find yourself, if you really want to be celibate, you can begin today by praying.[48]

Without prayer celibate chastity is hopeless; without hope it must lead to desperation and even degeneracy.

f) Community

In the monastic tradition chastity is lived in the context of a community. There are two aspects that may be considered here. In the first place a communitarian existence is necessarily organized independently of transient personal preferences. In most cases a general finality stamps itself on structures and activities so that once a common goal is recognized and chosen, no more is needed to progress towards that goal than to go with the flow. In a compatible community it is not necessary continually to stop and take sightings, and then to realign one's trajectory. Others are making the same journey as we. European monks conscripted into the army during the Second World War suddenly found it necessary to fight for their chastity on a different front when they moved from the monastery to the barracks. Only then did they realize how much help they received by living among brothers equally committed to becoming chaste: *bene instructi fraterna ex acie*—they were well taught by the fraternal ranks (1:5).

The community not only forms us in beliefs and values but also provides us with boundaries. It tells us how far we can go and when our behavior is beginning to move toward becoming either dangerous for ourselves or provocative and scandalous in the eyes of others. Since we ourselves probably are not fully aware of when we have wandered too far from the prudent and the ideal, we resent these limitations of our liberty and regard them as inapplicable. Beware. The very strength of the resentment is usually a sign that a word of caution was indeed necessary. Community standards can sometimes seem narrow but, even in that eventuality, they can serve as checks on our otherwise unexamined initiatives. Sometimes a willingness to conform to stricter expectations can save us from ourselves and from an unwilled disaster.

If we consider the monastic community as the Church in miniature, then our adherence to its principles and practices can carry with it something more than the rewards of conformity. There is grace to be found in the company and communion of believers. Here is a little story from a thirteenth-century handbook for Cistercian novices, putatively ascribed to Abbot Stephen of Sawley:

> One of our brothers, sitting alone and apart from the others during the rest period [at work], began to be gravely beset by temptations of the flesh; he heard a voice saying to him, "Go down to the camp." When he joined the others the temptation ceased.[49]

In the experience of many, difficulties with chastity begin with behavioral or affective separation from the community. This may be concealed for a time, and the living of a double life goes undetected, but eventually everything that is concealed is proclaimed from the rooftops. If the aberration is a momentary lapse from an otherwise honest life, then it can be rectified and the end result of the incident may be beneficial. If, on the other hand, the difficulty is compounded by years of compacted deceit and willfulness, there is little hope of a creative solution.

A good monastic community, however, does more to sustain chastity than provide us with rules and regulations to prevent its opposite. It is a place of acceptance, affirmation, support, friendship, and even some degree of intimacy. It is not meager with its celebration of gifts and its admiration of persons. It provides for all appropriate outlets for generativity. This is the ideal context in which to become chaste. Not a rigid impersonal system, nor an affective desert nor a riot of immature sentiment, but an atmosphere of solid adult mutuality, acceptance, and love. Paradoxically such ease in interpersonal existence is not easily gained. Nobody need think that such a fully affective community is easy to create or to live in. We arrive at such a state only by years of disciplined effort. Curiously enough, the undisciplined man or woman cannot survive in such a community; their own inner chaos will be projected upon the others to the extent that the goodness and holiness of the majority will not be apparent. To the affectively immature even the best community will seem seriously deficient.

There are numerous ersatz forms of intimacy that a genuinely affective community will not encourage or permit. Many people who enthuse about Aelred of Rievaulx's treatise *On Spiritual Friendship* have never grasped its message. The great gift of an intimate friendship is not the same as *un grand amour*. Aelred continues Cicero's theme that true friendship presupposes a high level of maturity and belongs especially to the mellower decades of life. Combined with the lightness of spirit that friendship confers, there is a certain gravitas of behavior that does not permit the relationship to degenerate into adolescent folly or anti-social exclusivity. Much less does it lay the foundation for genital interaction.

Over the years one who is in the process of becoming chaste will probably notice a burgeoning capacity for intimacy. With some more than others, certainly, but never with just one. Self-knowledge and a greater truthfulness brings with it an increased self-acceptance and a greater willingness to take the risk of self-exposure. An enlarged level of freedom from unconscious motivations makes us readier to do what we may never have done before, to reach out to other people, to welcome them into our inner space, and to be less afraid. This is why the saints had that quality of instant contact that politicians dream about. To meet someone who is genuinely holy is to have the impression of being both known and loved; no barrier is placed between persons. Heart speaks to heart.

Every step we make in the direction of inclusive intimacy is going to help us persevere in the practice of chastity. The monastic community can help us acquire this art: This is why the twelfth-century Cistercian unabashedly referred to the monastery as "a school of love." If our observance of the Rule does not carry us in this direction, there is something radically wrong. Community and chastity go hand in hand. We come to the monastery in order to learn to love, to put aside infantile narcissism and preoccupation with self, and to give scope to empathy and self-giving. One who lives thus is going to have comparatively few problems with the living of celibate chastity.

g) Personal Devotion to Christ

The early monks saw themselves as the successors to the martyrs. Because they had the misfortune to miss out on the possibility of shedding their blood in testimony to their faith in another sphere of existence, they were compelled to find other ways of pursuing otherworldliness. Monastic life may seem easier than being eaten by lions, but there are added hardships. To begin with, faithfully following a monastic call involves decades of fidelity to grace under changing circumstances. Instead of a once-and-for-all acceptance of a cruel fate it is death by a thousand pinpricks—felt all the more keenly because of the relative absence of compensating gratifications.

An important element of the spirituality of the martyrs, as revealed in the early narratives, was their passionate and personal devotion to Christ. It was this warm love rather than cool and calculating reason that helped them endure the hideous torments to which they were subjected. Both men and women eagerly looked forward to their death as a means of being united with Christ, whom they loved and ardently desired. This attitude flowed into the Rule and other early monastic texts to build up a conviction that the only appropriate motivation for embracing the rigors of monastic observance was a personal love for Christ and the sure and certain hope that this love will find its consummation in heaven.

Later we will have more to say about the centrality of this aspect of monastic spirituality. Let us concentrate here on the area of chastity. Since unchastity is habitually the effect of immature or disordered affectivity, it follows that harnessing the whole spiritual life to the task of growing in love—with the person of Jesus as an initial object of that love—is going to make the journey to love of a single piece with the other aspects of our spiritual endeavor. The dynamism of monastic life depends on our deciding the relative priority of different love-objects. This was referred to by the medieval Cistercian authors as the *ordinatio caritatis*. On this basis, fulfilling Benedict's injunction of placing nothing before the love of Christ (4:21) necessarily impacts on every other act which has love as its driving force. Our personal attachment to Christ becomes more important than any other relationship. As long as it flourishes it makes sure that no other relationship supplants it or gets out of control.

h) Purity of Heart

John Cassian cited purity of heart as the most appropriate object of monastic striving. By this expression he intended to convey the importance of simplicity of will. If the heart is divided in itself, then we cannot love God or our neighbor with our whole heart. We are not the masters of our own inner domain. The monastic endeavor is ultimately incompatible with half-heartedness. Hence the need, especially during the first decades of monastic striving, to bring some unity to our choices, progressively eliminating every inconsistency that has the potential to result in our leading double lives. We should be constantly asking ourselves why we entered the monastery and verifying that we are still animated by those initial desires. The more this basic finality governs our attitudes and choices, the more progress we make and the happier we are, despite the hard and rough patches that we encounter on our journey.

Purity of heart involves investing all our energies in a single venture, not allowing ourselves to become fragmented and confused. I cannot afford to be a part-time monk—this would mean that my monastic labors would never reach a critical mass, and the end result would be flatness and stagnation. Alternatively it would involve my attempting to live a double life, sometimes being a monk and at other times either a non-monk or an anti-monk. There may be an inherent excitement in such an attempt, but there is little permanent happiness. Monastic contentment usually depends on an attitude of "What You See Is What You Get": an attitude of sincere transparency that hides neither assets nor liabilities.

Such interior and exterior simplicity is especially beautiful in the area of sexual behavior, so often characterized by duplicity and lies. Allowing our lives to be as chaste as the monastic persona is both task and challenge, but it is the only way to be happy. Backsliding and compromises are dead-end streets that lead nowhere except to anxiety and eventual misery. In the long run, it makes more sense to live the kind of life to which we have committed ourselves, trusting that sustained fidelity to grace will in time yield its hundredfold.

i) Serenity

Embracing the ideals of the monastic vocation and simultaneously accepting our sexuality will help us to hold together the opposite ambitions of human nature and personal choice. Sometimes the battle is fierce between the contrary camps and the outcome by no means certain. In such a situation it is easy to become mentally confused and emotionally upset. Shame and guilt can prey upon our failures and drive us deep into such discouragement that we may consider cutting our losses. It is at such a point that we need to cultivate calm and serenity based on the theological virtue of hope. If we have not yet attained purity of heart at least we can make some progress toward peace of heart.

Many monasteries that follow Benedict's Rule emblazon the word *pax* or "peace" upon their portals. To many outsiders the undoubtedly peaceful atmosphere they encounter in such holy places is a result of a quiet life untouched by cares or conflicts. Those who live there know differently. Peace is certainly a gift of the Holy Spirit, but it also profits from human exertion. Newcomers to a monastery are often surprised that they have to work hard to avoid becoming upset. For anything much to happen at a spiritual level a certain amount of groundwork has to be done in acquiring the skills of emotional literacy and management, honest communication, and conflict resolution. Such arts help to lubricate community living.

On a personal and interior level we also need to acquire certain skills or attitudes. Chief among these is the relinquishing of any ambition to control what is happening in our spiritual life. This means accepting the inevitable wobbliness of our will and the futility of trying to mastermind our own journey to God. Somewhere along the road we have to learn to trust, and the sooner the better. We may give lip-service to the saying that God can write straight on crooked lines, but continue to hope that in our own case it will not be necessary

Nothing is more distressing to a relatively innocent soul that failure in chastity. Because we do not speak frankly enough about our experience of sexuality, many monastic people assume that their own liabilities in this area are uncommonly serious. Sometimes their education to celibacy has been incomplete and often they lack the vocabulary to engage in serious discourse about what is happening. Some of these defects *may* have been addressed and reduced during the time of formation, but most people continue to hope desperately that they will not have to cope with serious sexual issues, that somehow they will be exempt from normality.

Sexuality, like every other aspect of our experience, must be covered with the mantle of serenity. It is very unlikely that our lifelong journey toward chastity will be without mishap, be it of thought, desire, or deed. There will certainly be temptations, and often we will not evade them quickly enough to avoid being tarnished by them. Memories and images can remain embedded in our subconscious for years, only too ready to rise and taunt us in idle moments. Even though our conduct is beyond reproach, we know that our thoughts and desires have often betrayed us. If we were a little more convinced that this is more the norm than the exception, perhaps we could survey the situation with greater serenity.

The fundamental fact is that it does not much matter whether our failings and fallings are many or few. Our confidence and our peace stem from our being convinced that God's love for us is unconditional. This is not to say that our sins do not matter. It is simply to assert that whatever barriers we interpose between ourselves and God they are too insubstantial to stand for long. Our sexual failures are no different from our other sins, even though they may occasion a deeper feeling of shame. God can use our sense of their seriousness to demonstrate that even the offenses we most regret are no more than specks of dust on the scales of mercy. Trust in God is the only unfailing source of serenity.

j) Contemplation

The ancient monks were convinced that chastity and contemplation went hand in hand. To understand what they are saying, it has to be remembered that they distinguished between mere continence, or the lack of overt sexual activity, and the radiant inner light of chastity. Contemplation is neither achievement nor the reward of achievement but a gift of God. It occurs most readily in a heart that is undivided and fixed in its conformity with the divine will. God, however, sometimes breaks his own rules and gives this gift not at the end of the spiritual ascent, but on the way up. By giving the struggling wayfarer a foretaste of what lies at the end of the journey, God motivates and energizes the process of coming to a more complete chastity.

Chastity is probably impossible without serious commitment to prayer, and serious commitment to prayer leads to the sort of ordering of life which facilitates contemplation. There does not seem much point in trying to analyze the details of this causality; experience confirms that there is a connection, though it is not without elements of paradox.

k) Never Lose Hope in the Mercy of God (4:74).

Benedict is not known as a great practical joker. It appears to me, however, that he was leading us up the garden path by listing no less than seventy-two implements of good work that we are expected to use throughout our long life, because he then adds a final one that seems to negate all those industrious decades. After prescribing so many good works he reverts to a purer gospel that bids us only to have faith and hope, and never to doubt the generosity or large-heartedness of God.

For some the loss of sexual innocence has been the occasion of the discovery of mercy; for others an ingrained habit or persistent need has taught them dependence on this same mercy. In the light of such experiences it seems as though the difficulty that many experience in maintaining chastity is a providential means of learning the more important message that the spiritual life is not a matter of achievement but of being the recipient of God's benevolence. "It is a matter not of the one who wills nor of the one who runs but of God showing mercy" (Rom. 9:16). So long as chastity seems to be achievable without God, it has no relevance in Christian discipleship. In fact it is probably an obstacle. On the contrary, chastity lost or threatened is sometimes the best thing that can happen to a fervent follower in Benedict's footsteps.

6 | *Dispossession*

*He must keep for himself nothing
of all he owned.*
RB 58:24

Just as chastity is viewed by secularized cultures as an
impediment to human fulfillment, so it is not surprising
to find that very few persons living on our planet today
are indifferent to the prospect of accumulating possessions.
Whether we are rich or poor most of us were raised to be
seriously concerned about acquiring new wealth and making
sure that it is not taken from us. Although we live in a world
choking on consumer goods, shopping malls are thronged
with people hoping to fill an inner emptiness with yet more
items fondly believed to be life-enhancing. Notwithstanding
the existence of an underclass that struggles to maintain a
minimum level of decency and respectability, and which
easily slips into real neediness, the self-image of most
Western societies is of a culture of affluence and conspicuous
expenditure. If we were cynics we might imagine that the
world would end not with a bang, nor with a whimper, but
with the sound of cash registers celebrating the success of the
end-of-the-world sales.

Against such a backdrop the choice to be "poor with the
poor Christ" and "naked to follow the naked Christ" must

seem to many the height of folly. Even for those who enter a monastery, the demands of dispossession can be muted. St. Benedict did not insist on absolute poverty, but relied on principles of necessity, sufficiency, and moderation, and on avoiding proprietary attitudes by insisting on community of goods, minimizing acquisitiveness by giving to all what they genuinely needed, and conforming to common sense by recognizing a sliding scale in assessing individual needs.

As a result it is possible to dodge the demands of poverty unless we have a certain clarity of vision about its essential role in the monastic process.

1. Material Poverty

Unless the monastery is one of those rare establishments that is actually impoverished and has made strenuous efforts over the years to remain so, monks and nuns scarcely feel the pinch of poverty beyond artificial restrictions placed on expenditure. Monasteries accumulate money fairly easily, sometimes because of the generosity of donors, sometimes because of favorable taxation status, but often through a combination of hard work and frugal living. As a result there is no fundamental fear for the future, or even the sobriety that comes with having to skimp now in order to set by a little for later. Compared with so many exploited workers, recipients of welfare, chronic invalids, and those who are just unlucky, the monastic standard of living is comfortable enough. Moreover, unless they are explicitly challenged, many recruits bring into the monastery the same acquisitive presuppositions that motivated their choices outside. "They wish to be poor in such a way that nothing is lacking to them. They love poverty so long as they experience no shortage."[50] As a result they bear with ill grace a lower standard of living than they had before entry and are constantly exerting pressure that everything become "a little nicer."

Such unprincipled ameliorism is more destructive of the monastic spirit than appears at first glance. It bespeaks a heart and mind set on temporal convenience and not striving to become worthy citizens of heaven. There are some members of monastic communities who are highly diligent in discerning vocations, states of prayer, and potential candidates for the abbacy who do not apply the same discernment to the area of monastic poverty. Most monks and nuns expect to eat well. Many will not tolerate any reservation or hesitation when it comes to upgrading furnishings, appliances, and equipment. There are those who have little concern about energy expenditure and others who would prefer to lose a limb than to have any restriction placed on their automobile use. I would never choose a situation that habitually threatened chastity, but I do not seem to feel the same reluctance to ignore the exigencies of monastic poverty. Maybe I unconsciously assume that a comfortable bourgeois lifestyle is my right, some kind of compensation for the rigors of celibacy: a consolation prize.

Even the dimmest knowledge of monastic history leads to the conclusion that the love of practical poverty is one of the surest gauges of fervor. Troubles often multiply when monasteries become rich and the monks' status and standard of living creep inexorably upward. "The association of possessions and virtues is not usually long-lasting."[51] I say this not unaware of the complexities of economic survival as it concerns monastic communities in today's world. And I am certainly not recommending a tight-fisted niggardliness in dealing with requests. Such an attitude is contrary to the genial spirit of *humanitas* that pervades Benedict's Rule. It is good to remember, however, that while attending to the special needs of "the weak," Benedict expects the rest of the community to soldier on without resentment, keeping to the stricter observance as the path that will lead more directly to their goal. To arrive at a situation where the majority is classified as technically infirm in order to justify a looser observance conforms neither to the letter nor to the spirit of monastic tradition.[52] Certainly, from the Cistercian end of the Benedictine spectrum, austerity of life remains both a characteristic and a priority. This strictness necessarily includes the pinch of voluntary poverty.

Monastic poverty is neither glamorous nor romantic. It is a matter of choosing to go without, to make do with less, and to be content with little. In the eyes of most of our contemporaries it is not a goal worth pursuing. It is ugly and contemptible. Bernard compares poverty to dung; it may increase growth, but of itself it is repulsive.[53] Real poverty in buildings and their furnishings is not the same as an aesthetic minimalism, which is usually quite expensive. Rather it involves using what is plain and commonplace—sometimes, everything else being equal, deliberately opting for what is cheap. The aura that undoubtedly pervades monastic building comes from decades of prayer and holiness, and not merely from a first-rate architect and an unlimited budget. What Benedict says in speaking of monastic clothing can be taken as indicative of a general attitude. Apart from serving its purpose and fitting those who wear it, clothing should be chosen on the basis of what is locally available and what is less expensive—not imported from afar, no status brand names and high price tags: the sort of clothes that no respected denizen of the worldly city would want to be seen wearing. Benedict and the monastic reformers who followed him sought to deprive clothes and everything else that constitutes the monastic lifestyle of secular collateral meanings. Clothes were simply coverings for the body; they were not intended to express superiority or status. Food was meant to sustain energy levels so as to make monastic observance possible; it was not to become an end in itself, a gratification of gluttony, or a compensation for celibacy. Buildings were simply places in which to live, not museums or academies or country clubs, but extra-territorial islands where everything was determined according to monastic priorities, *pro modo conversationis* (22:2).

What are you thinking as you read this? Are you not conscious of a certain reluctance or resistance to a radical interpretation of monastic poverty? I am conscious of it in myself as I write; I hear the voices of common sense, practicality, and efficiency crying out to be heard. Even our Western monastic tradition raises its voice in protest: "We are followers of Benedict, not Francis!" Yet the quiet voice of the gospel insists. The following of Jesus demands detachment from and indifference to material possessions. Is the maxim about a camel passing through the eye of a needle really saying to us that monastic life will be almost impossible without a solid practice of poverty? As with chastity, if we make compromises in the area of poverty the integrity of monastic observance is lost, and every element in it is forced to operate at a reduced level of vitality. The more substantial the failures, the more fragmented our efforts seem to become, and the integrity of our response to vocation is ripped further apart. Monastic life becomes unsustainable without a solid commitment to both personal and communal poverty.

Monastic poverty is not merely a matter of spending less or even of being content with the basic necessities, a few conveniences, and relatively rare extravagances. Owning high-quality goods bespeaks a certain worthiness in the possessor. If I live in a beautiful monastery set on prime real estate, if I am surrounded by good art and an ambience of high culture, then, when I announce myself as belonging to such a place, I am immediately invested with some of its prestige. Like Paul (in Acts 21:39) I can boast, "I am a monk of no mean monastery." People often judge the quality of monastic life by externals. A genuinely poor monastery may excite admiration, but it frightens away prospective candidates.[54] And, oddly enough, such a place does not appeal to many benefactors as worthy of their largesse.

"For some unknown reason, the richer a place appears, the more freely do offerings pour in."[55] The poverty to which the followers of Benedict aspire has no fringe benefits. It is not aimed at exciting the admiration of pious observers. It is simply expressive of the fact that those who live in monasteries have different goals and different priorities. They are citizens of the heavenly city; it is there that their treasures are located. Voluntary self-deprivation, doing without the goods and services that much money provides, and renouncing competitive consumption, taken together indicate that major importance is attached to non-material realities.

Benedict's teaching on hospitality takes monastic poverty beyond the confines of renunciation into the sphere of faith and largeness of heart. All strangers are not only to be welcomed as Christ himself, but Christ is to be adored in them by a manifest sign of reverence (53:7). Special diligence is to apply in the reception of poor people and travelers, lest faith-inspired kindness be watered down by our tendency to dismiss such persons as unworthy of our full attention. Benedict dryly adds that the terror inspired by the rich and powerful is sufficient to ensure that they are received with the honor and respect worthy of their rank (53:15). If we were really indifferent to material wealth then we would treat everyone like millionaires.

Benefactors and founders have played an important role in the spread of monasticism, at least in the West. Monastic communities often earn enough to live on, but the fact that they can only work part-time means that they have to rely on Providence for capital expenditure and, more important, for means to cover the expense involved in making new foundations. It is natural that such generous people are welcomed with greater enthusiasm than others. Natural, yes, but not necessarily in accordance with the spirit of the gospel or the teaching of the Rule. I am not saying that we should treat benefactors less well, but that we should ensure that our respect and affection are directed toward persons and not to their money, exactly the same as in the case of the poor.

Sometimes it happens that particular monks and nuns develop a talent for acquiring personal benefactors who provide them with goods and services that are unavailable through normal channels in the community. This can be from those who are grateful for what they receive from the monastery or from family or personal friends. Benedict is aware of this tactic and is uncompromising in his rejection of it. Immediately after the chapter on the welcoming of strangers he adds one that prohibits monks from receiving unauthorized gifts, be they ever so small or pious (54:1–5). Elsewhere he forbids them to accept meals when outside the monastery, no matter how pressing the invitation (51:1). In most cultures reciprocity rules such areas as hospitality and gift-giving. When the monk or nun receives others, they do so in the name of the community. To use that service as a means of building up a sense of personal indebtedness in the recipients of monastic hospitality is to usurp for personal profit what rightly belongs to the community as a whole.

> a) Letting it be known that we are open to receive gifts from those outside the community can lead to a preferential option for the rich. We pay more attention to those who can do favors for us, who can give us presents, or who can bestow certain intangible assets such as love, esteem, affirmation, and admiration. As a result we become exploiters. We see others only in terms of potential advantage for ourselves. Real friends, both personal and community, respect our vocation and its concrete exigencies. They do not want to do anything that would weaken its integrity.
>
> b) When we receive gifts, especially extravagant gifts, a certain indebtedness is created. We can be reasonably sure that in some subtle way we will

be expected to reciprocate. We do this by giving more of our time and attention, by diverting community resources in favor of the donor, or even by compromising some of the principles of monastic behavior that ought to remain permanently intact.

c) When some members of a community, whether by virtue of their position or their personality, seem to receive and retain many gifts, especially when these are of a kind not available to others, a climate of inequality develops. When secret assets are shared among a few, the possessor is in a position to exercise patronage—to invite to his parties those whom he chooses and to exclude those whom he rejects. This kind of behavior is liable to lead to serious problems, as Benedict notes (69:1–4).

d) Monastic poverty involves a certain solidarity, if not with the poorest of the poor, at least with ordinary working-class people. This means that we ought to be diffident about accepting the little luxuries that kind-hearted friends often delight in pressing upon us. Occasional treats probably do no harm, but when these are institutionalized, they lead to a situation in which we come to expect that we drink only fine wines and wear only well-cut and fashionable clothes. More important, when, for some reason we are compelled to lower our standards, we become upset. Our emotional investment in such relative luxuries indicates that our hearts are divided.

e) Monastic life is impossible without attention given to the preservation of symbols. Often our principles are made visible and reinforced only because they are expressed to us and to others by certain material tokens. A neatly patched habit, for example, reminds us and others that we have opted out of consumerism and are happy to make the most of what we have. The absence of the latest gadgets tells everyone that we are living on a different planet—which, in a sense, is true. It is no great tragedy if our meals remind us that we are more like Lazarus sitting at the gate than the rich man who feasted magnificently every day, since this animates our hope that we too will be called to Abraham's bosom.

Monastic poverty should not be thought of as being imposed from the top and resignedly accepted by the rank and file. In that case much ingenuity will be exercised in subverting official parsimony by all sorts of demeaning subterfuges. If poverty is not only practised but also loved, then life becomes less cluttered, and more of our energy can be directed to seeking that for which we came to the monastery in the first place.

2. Poverty of Spirit

Material poverty is important, but humility is essential for perseverance in monastic life. Without poverty of spirit no purity of heart is possible. Here we understand this quality less as a feature of social living and more as an attitude toward ourselves. Do we live in full awareness of the liabilities we carry? Just as chastity can be built only on a foundation of truth, so poverty is really a matter of stripping away the distraction of material wealth, which hides our nothingness from ourselves and others. Expensive possessions may signal to others that we are people of substance, but the signal is wrong. Naked we came into the world and from it we will depart naked; everything that obscures that truth is an obstacle to true humanity.

That humility was important for Benedict is obvious from the amount of space he devoted to it. It is the longest chapter in the Rule.[56] Humility is a gospel quality that is particularly difficult for our contemporaries—on the one hand we live in an age of blatant self-promotion and, on the other, never before have so many people suffered from the baneful effects of an unhealthily low self-esteem. This means that practising humility, as Benedict understood it, demands a solid conversion of mind and heart. Our beliefs and values are framed in the context of the gospel promise of ultimate reversal. If we wish to be high we must be low. If we wish to be first we must be last. If we desire to flower and bear fruit, then, paradoxically, we must seek the environment of the desert.

The spirit of poverty that restricts our use and consumption of material goods also inclines us to have no more than a moderate degree of self-appreciation. In particular, it calls on us to affirm our dependence on God for all that is good, even for our own spiritual progress. This means recognizing that when it comes to consistency in the matter of the spiritual disciplines we are fairly unreliable. Most of us cannot afford to be frivolous in spiritual matters; we have to work hard to maintain the intensity of our search for God. What inspires this sobriety is our recognition of the part sin has played in our personal history; who and what we are today has been tainted by our resistance to grace and our willful choices—invisible though this may be to our friends and admirers.

If you read through Benedict's chapter on humility you will notice that most of the behavior patterns he praises are utterly repugnant to modern sensibilities: fear of God, submission, patient acceptance of injustice, a preference for what is cheap, self-denigration, conformity, silence, and seriousness. And how hard it is for us to appreciate the values embodied in Benedict's portrayal of a monk who has ascended to the very top of the ladder: He is always conscious of his sins and dreads the judgment; his prayer has not risen above the publican's plea for mercy. Before we see this as an ideal there has to be a massive shift in our values.

Curiously, most of the saints seem instinctively to have understood the necessity of poverty of spirit. Sometimes we are surprised that they were so modest in their self-appreciation. Some, like St. Thérèse of Lisieux seem to have created a whole system based on littleness. Many of the saints have been bold, but few of them were bombastic, particularly in self-presentation. Their message was the Good News of God's love—they were not marketing themselves. They were sincere when they spoke of themselves as unworthy stewards and unprofitable servants. They were not obsessed with sin, but they had a clear eye that enabled them to perceive their own proneness to evil. This clarity of vision came from an overwhelming conviction that God's love was unconditional. In a sense their own lamentable failures did not much matter to them, and so they were never forced into denial and repression.

We are unlikely to come to an appreciation of the role of humility in the Benedictine tradition unless we have disenfranchised ourselves from contemporary Western culture. And we are unlikely to become strangers to the ways of the world unless we have some intuition about the role that humility plays in preparing us to meet God. Maintaining our distinctiveness and cultivating the humility typical of the monastic charism go hand in hand. You will not find one without the other.

3. The Fragility of Life

If we depart from the sphere of moral endeavor and move into more neutral territory we will discover that we humans live in a very precarious situation. "This world is most appropriately called the land of the dying because in it nothing is stable, nothing eternal and the life of human beings is lived in the shadow of death."[57] None of us is certain about what tomorrow will bring. Apart from the remote possibility of an asteroid strike that will render us as extinct as the dinosaurs, there are many factors that threaten the continued existence of the human species. See how much we have degraded the earth on the groundless assumption that ecological damage is self-repairing. How easily we lull ourselves into lethal inactivity by believing that there is no urgency. Look at the low moral caliber of most national leaders and the callous stupidity and self-interest of the populations that elect them. Is there any folly of which, we can confidently assert, they are not capable? If television is a reliable guide to intelligence and interests of peoples, a disinterested observer would have to wonder whether there is any hope at all for the future.

Since the nineteenth century we have been half-convinced by the myth of progress so that we half-believe that tomorrow will be better than today. A glance at history should disabuse us of that notion. It is not only the prospect of plagues, famines, and natural disasters that ought to occasion a sobering apprehension. There are also the deliberate or unforeseen effects of political choices: wars, rampant injustice, disempowerment, discrimination, persecution. We are right if we are somewhat concerned about the morrow and its quality of life.

Even if global disasters are averted, there is no guarantee that tragedy will not strike our own lives and those of the people we love. Every day there are fatal accidents, terminal diagnoses, the break-up of relationships, the loss of employment, the failure of cherished projects. None of us is so lucky that we have no experience of such adversities. The world that we have so carefully constructed around us teeters constantly on the brink of extinction. To the extent that we have mortgaged our happiness to the continuance of the status quo, one day we will probably face a major crisis.

If such considerations fail to move us perhaps we should turn our attention to the certainty of death.[58] This is, of course, the ultimate act of dispossession. Not only do we retain for ourselves nothing of what we previously owned, but from that day onward we do not have any power over the material elements that hitherto constituted our own body (58:24-25). It is not only death, but the years of vital attrition and the progressive diminishment that precede it. As I write I am sixty-two years old; this means that in all probability three-quarters of my life has finished and what remains is likely to be inhibited by impairment. Obviously, I do not much like this. It is, however, a reality. What it means for me is that I had better hurry up and get started on doing the things I want to have done during my lifetime. For the night comes when no one can do any work.

And so, whether we voluntarily anticipate death by self-dispossession or whether we cling tightly until the last moment, at the end we are all called to detachment not only from material realities but from bodily instincts and eventually from the body and from life itself. Those of us familiar with monastic customs are probably aware that death is, in a way, anticipated by the ritual of monastic profession.[59] In entering a monastery and committing ourselves to spend the rest of our life there we are, in a sense, dying to the world—just as in baptism. If Martin Heidegger could define the human person as "a being-towards-death," then surely this definition must apply even more fully to the monk. Benedict, we know, sees the daily remembrance of death as a spur to fidelity (4:47). And it is probably true that death is a regular visitor to most established monasteries—with the ancient monastic rituals surrounding it offering little scope to hide its finality. To sit in silent vigil beside the body of one who was so recently alive brings home the reality of the end that awaits us all. It is only a matter of time before it is my turn. In some monasteries the church door leading to the cemetery

was inscribed with the words *Ille hodie et ego cras*. Today
he: tomorrow me.

Our Christian faith, however, keeps reminding us that
death is the doorway to eternal life, so that there is no need
to attempt to blot it out of consciousness. In fact one of
the high points of monastic profession is the triple chant
of the *Suscipe*: "Receive me, O Christ, according to your
promise and I shall live; do not disappoint me of my hope."
This is not only an apt verse for profession, but a wonderful accompaniment for the transition to eternal life. I hope
someone remembers to sing it for me on my deathbed. And
it is an equally wonderful mantra all life long. We live in
hope (4:41), ardently desiring eternal life (4:46) and never
despairing of the mercy of God (4:74). With so much to
hang onto, it is not so difficult to let go of lesser benefits

It is eschatological hope that allows the monk to take
present reverses less seriously and to hanker less intensely
for the conveniences and gratifications that will last only
for a time. This attitude derives not from a negativity about
created reality in itself, but from the recognition that when
affections and desires become fixated at a level below the
optimum, one's whole personhood is devalued and one's
sensibility is debased. Surgeons and pianists and others
whose hands are crucial to them should not work in a timber
mill. An accident would cause them to lose more than their
fingers—in a sense, without the means of self-expression,
their spirit would be quenched. Monastic tradition is
formed around a firm faith that as human beings we are
intended for union with God. Nothing else can fully satisfy
us. To allow ourselves to be diverted by the pursuit of
temporal realities in such a way that our spiritual energies
are diminished is ultimately self-diminishing.

In fact, letting go is a means of liberation. "Freedom's
just another word for nothing left to lose"[60]—at least,
according to a popular song of the 1970s. It is true that
many possessions can become burdensome because of the

care needed to maintain them and the anxiety that accompanies potential loss. Reducing our involvement with them allows our energies to be channeled in other directions. Poverty is more than economic abstemiousness. It is a work of faith, calling us to be less interested in things of earth and time, and to invest more of our resources in eternity. It is to give priority to the unseen. What is seen is corruptible and soon passes away. What is unseen endures for ever. Those who cling to what is eternal are not poor. They are endowed with the only riches worth having.

7 | *Antecedent Willingness*

The benefit of obedience
RB 71:1

In a world that cherishes autonomy and self-assertion the monastic ideal of obedience seems both oppressive and unhealthy, akin to the dehumanizing systems that shape the societies in which we live. It is not so easy to see obedience as a spiritual dynamism that is an essential component of all Christian discipleship and that has a direct bearing on the quality of our prayer. As a result those entering monasteries often carry with them negative attitudes that lead them to confront the reality of obedience with a mere compliance that will often degenerate into a surly minimalism. This is especially true of those entering from a background that is consistently suspicious of governments, resentful of bosses, and reluctant to follow rules and regulations. For such people, unless somebody takes the trouble to educate them, monastic obedience is purgatorial at best and, at worst, a veritable hell on earth.

The fact is that, even in a monastery, obedience can become infected with beliefs and values that transform it into something far different from what Benedict intended. Something is lost when monastic texts about obedience are interpreted merely as recommendations that we do what a superior commands. In that case the monk's life would be reduced to the level of a canine obedience school or the army. The primary function of obedience is ascetical, not organizational. The real action takes place at the level of belief and value: That is why Benedict insists on the primary role of *doctrina* and *disciplina* in the exercise of authority. This is to take up a New Testament idea that obedience is more a **state** than an **action**; it is closely identified with faith.[61] Obedience is, in the first place, an antecedent openness, an attitude of receptivity, a willingness to listen combined with the recognition that this responsiveness may involve changing one's life in accordance with what one hears. It is the attitude of the girl keeping the gate in Acts 12:13—alert and listening so that she can answer a summons promptly.

1. God or Self?

Monastic obedience presupposes that we have elected to give priority to the divine will over our own. This is why, in his ladder of humility, Benedict places the abandonment of self-will and a more general submission to the divine will before he moves to cenobitic obedience (7:31–34). Rendering obedience to an abbot is one specific form by which the monk imitates the self-emptying of Christ. The general attitude goes beyond interaction between subject and superior, even beyond mutual obedience: It is an unrestricted search for God's will. Such an attitude is incumbent on everyone in the monastery, including superiors. This is why abbots are to ask counsel of the young (3:3), and to pay attention to any criticisms offered by a visiting monk (61:4). In both cases it is Christ who speaks through human agents—the less overpowering they are, the more attentively the abbot must strain to hear what they say. The same principle applies here that Benedict enunciates concerning the poor: The terror that great ones inspire assures them of respect (53:15), but it is in listening carefully to the little people, the young, the marginalized, and the inarticulate, that Christ is more especially honored. Even the scoundrels of the community, supposing that there be some, are to be heard, since they often read situations more acutely than those blindly committed to the preservation of the status quo.

Dorotheos of Gaza makes the same point. God always reveals what is best, provided we are prepared to hear the divine voice in the most unlikely place. He cites as an example Balaam's donkey (Num. 22:22–34). If God can speak through a donkey, how much more likely is it that even the least important among the faithful might be carriers of his word? It is not the speaking of God's revealing word that is in doubt, it is our capacity to hear it.

> In the same way do not ponder what you have to do if you have no one from whom you may ask [counsel]. God will not abandon any who wholeheartedly seek to know God's will in truth. God will in everything show them the way according to his will. For those who turn their heart to God's will God will enlighten a little child to speak his will.[62]

Such listening has an element of vigilance in it. Its greatest enemy is not rebellion or rejection but inattention. We can easily be distracted by dominant cares and anxieties so that we forget to pay attention to the messages that life brings us, in events and the actions of others as well as in words. Somehow or other our concentration relaxes and our powers of attention are not engaged. Like the goats at the final judgment we protest that we were unaware of the challenges presented to us, but, frighteningly, this excuse is invalid. As Benedict's first step of humility reminds us, it is our task to remain focused on finding God's will and conforming to it. This is a proactive form of listening, constantly cocking our ears for the slightest sound as if our life depended on it—as indeed it does.

The attitude of listening evoked in the first word of the Rule is typified in the monk's response to the signal for the Work of God. Remember that there were no private timepieces. As soon as a monk heard the signal, he was to drop whatever was in hand, and run quickly yet gravely to respond (43:1). In the Middle Ages the bell that summoned the community to the various exercises was regarded as *vox Dei*—the voice of God. Coming late is reprehensible not merely as an expression of personal sloppiness, nor even as an act of disrespect to the gathered community, but because it indicates a slowness in responding to God's call. Moreover in many cases such tardiness indicates a willful preference for the private activity of an individual over the divinely sanctioned program of the *coenobium*.

To extrapolate from this particular instance, it seems likely that a monk's openness to God's voice in the events of daily life is probably a good indicator of the level of receptivity with which he approaches his prayer and *lectio divina*, his spiritual direction, and his interpretation of daily events. If he consistently resists challenge or change and is truculent and intransigent in his dealings with those in authority, it is scarcely believable that he is much different in his relationship with God. One who will not listen to Moses and the prophets will find plenty of excuses to dispute the authenticity of God's call, no matter how imposing the channels of revelation. A wholesome attitude of receptivity is usually indivisible. In listening, it does not distinguish between major superiors and minor superiors, between seniors and juniors, between fervent and marginal. It is prepared to believe that anybody can be a messenger of God, even Balaam's donkey.

If genuine obedience is considered primarily as a state or even an attitude, then its absence can be invisible. Apart from occasional crises there may be no outright rejection of orders—simply avoidance and defensiveness. Such monks or nuns may think themselves blameless in the matter of obedience, and, in a sense, they are—provided that superiors sense the situation and ensure that they remain at a safe distance. Not to be disobedient is not necessarily to be obedient. To harvest the benefits of genuine obedience more is required than avoiding overt rebellion. Nowadays if we do not actively seek obedience, years may pass without our being given any opportunity to practise it. If we give superiors and others such a hard time that they go out of their way to avoid asking anything of us, we can scarcely claim to have fulfilled either the purpose or spirit of our monastic profession. If we construct our life so that large areas of it are protected by firewalls from external demands, then it may be a worthy life, but it is not necessarily one that is free of the tyranny of self-will.

For Benedict liberation from self-will is the primary purpose of monastic obedience.[63] He addresses his words only to those who wish to serve Christ through the renunciation of self-will and the practice of obedience (Prol. 3). In Chapter 5, "On Obedience," he gives a phenomenological description of how a perfect disciple practises obedience.[64] For most of us this would seem like an impossible ideal. Benedict, however, locates such immediate compliance within the affective context of eschatological desire. Such disciples are "those whom love obliges to keep walking toward eternal life." If we truly seek the realities that are above, then we will have a corresponding lack of interest in getting our own way in matters that are of earth. Benedict continues:

> And so they grasp the narrow path of which
> the Lord said, "Narrow is the path that leads
> to life." They desire to live in coenobia with an
> abbot over them so that they do not live by their
> own assessment or obey their own desires and
> pleasures, but walk by another's judgment and
> rule. (5:11-12)

In other words, people come to a monastery in order
to find the possibility of obedience. Obedience is not an
unavoidable by-product of communal living to be endured
and tolerated. Obedience is the purpose and soul of the
monastic organization; the primacy is not the other way
around. Cenobitic life is, in Benedict's view, superior to the
life of a solitary precisely because it offers more opportunity
for the monk to be formed and strengthened by creative
interaction (1:5). In practice this demands submission to
others.

The self-will that obedience combats is a perverse will that
is extravagantly attached to self-maintenance and self-
gratification. It has no experience of falling in love with
anything outside itself. It does not know what it means to
forget itself and lose itself in loving admiration of another.
It stubbornly refuses any invitation to transcendence. It
is imperious in its demand for instant compliance; any
resistance will provoke moodiness, temper tantrums, and
bouts of sulky depression. Think of Ahaz when Naboth
frustrated his plans (1 Kings 21:4). Self-will is not only
directed to self-indulgence and worldly behavior. It may
well thrive within the limitations and obligations of
monastic life if they happen to suit, but, mysteriously,
despite strict observance not much real progress in interior
monasticity occurs. One who is dominated by self-will
cannot become Christlike.

What is so wrong with self-will? Benedict understands
that the interior promptings that often drive us to action

are often suspect. We should beware of their destructive potential: "There are paths which seem humanly right whose end plunges into the depths of hell" (7:21). The danger of self-will is that it blinds us to the real meaning of our actions—we lose the capacity to evaluate issues in the light of the gospel. Listen to what Benedict says about the Sarabites, the sort of monks who feel no necessity to be bound by either a rule or by the experience of a master or shepherd. "The pleasure of their desires is their law: whatever they think or choose they call holy, and what they do not want to do they consider illicit" (1:9). In such a case what is done may, in fact, be holy, and what is not done may be well-avoided. That is not the point. Benedict's contention is that such actions lack the guarantee of authenticity. As John Cassian would say, they are gold that has not been authoritatively assayed. As a result, energy may be wasted, for instance, by investing huge effort in something that is, at best, indifferent. Even worse, what seems like a good idea may eventually cause damage. Monastic life is a marathon and not a sprint; only those who run the full race are eligible for the prize.

Generally what happens is that the temptation to self-will initially has as its object behavior that is virtuous beyond the common norm. A young monk may well adopt practices of mortification that deprive him of sleep or food or necessary recreation. As a corollary he begins to regard the common standards as defective, and those who observe them as lacking in fervor. Counsel is not sought, pastoral intervention, is not welcomed and sometimes an element of secretiveness is present. The ascetic practices adopted at the behest of self-will have the effect of isolating the foolish fellow from the usual sources of fraternal or pastoral help. He is now on his own. Who is surprised when sudden temptation looms and he is dramatically overcome?[65] "There are paths which seem humanly right whose end plunges into the depths of hell." This is why Benedict, in his chapter on Lent, advises the monk to check out his proposed program of Lenten abnegation with the abbot; if he is acting from self-will he may simply be expressing and reinforcing his vices rather than neutralizing them (49:8–10). Self-will and vainglory go hand in hand.

When the ancient monks were confronted with the reality that often a highly persuasive temptation seems to come from nowhere, they concluded that it was demonic in origin. As a result the poor old devil has been blamed for many things going wrong in which he or she had no involvement. We post-Freudians, who have a smattering of knowledge about the workings of the unconscious mind, are reasonably familiar with the idea that we can be strongly inclined towards a particular course of action without our being fully aware of what it is that attracts us. Instinctively we disguise our desires with a semblance of rationality and deny the overt meaning of what we want to do. Anyone else could tell us that our behavior is self-indulgent or self-destructive, but we are blind to its true nature. Despite all our self-exculpating bluster, the fact is that we can easily become accomplices in our own troubles if we do not take care to impose a moratorium on our impulsive desires and learn to live according to an external standard: to conform our lives to an authoritative rule, an experienced pastor, and a community of fellow-travelers on the road to eternal life. Such an obedience blocks the automatic implementation of the whims of self-will and offers the possibility that our limited energies will be expended in areas where they will be most likely to yield fruit.

2. Laying the Foundation

Many, and perhaps all, bring into the monastery problems with authority that were generated in early life. A response to authority can be anything between exhibiting a puppy-like desire to please and going all the way to childish reluctance and passive aggression. Resistance and rebellion, likewise, can be merely verbal, or they may represent something more serious: instinctive or habitual rejection of authority, adolescent truculence, or the expression of a severe personality disorder. A negative attitude toward authority, whatever form it takes, whether conscious or unconscious, and of whatever degree, poses a particular problem for formation. If a young monk or nun lacks the necessary disposition for profiting from the very special role that authority is supposed to play in a monastery, then the whole process of internalization of values is jeopardized, and their future monastic prospects look dim.

To arrive at a wholesome degree of self-knowledge takes time. Meanwhile we have to live without it. Either we can choose blindly to act out our particular inclinations, or we can enter into an apprenticeship by which we learn how to read our experience and how to channel our affective energies so that they contribute to our progress toward the goal we have set before ourselves. This latter option means we accept to be disciples and submit ourselves to an instructor.

At first we may be aware only of the negative aspects of submission—the habitual nonimplementation of our personal preferences, and the labor involved in scrutinizing our motivations and the humiliation of being prepared to render an account of them. No more carefree living! Here Benedict seeks to motivate us by pointing to the example of Christ's self-emptying (5:13, 7:32, 7:34). To allow others to govern us is a basic component of the imitation of Christ. This is particularly true, as Guerric of Igny points out, when those to whom we submit are inferior to us.[66] This is probably how we feel, although it may not be true. We may feel that we know better than the one placed over us, but we walk in Christ's footsteps if we put aside our sense of superiority, at least for the moment, and submit.

In English the word "master" has a double reference. On the one hand it points to someone who exercises practical supervision over our behavior, who gives us instructions about what to do and how to do it. Our response is to serve. On the other hand a master also imparts theoretical knowledge, expands our minds, and teaches us. Our response is to learn. In a community that follows Benedict's rule both *doctrina* and *disciplina* are to be found: The community imparts both theory and practice to the newcomer and seeks to maintain a high level of both in all its members. Accordingly, those called to exercise some authority in the community must be skilled in doctrine; they are not put in charge simply to give orders. In Benedict's mind they must also be able effectively to communicate the beliefs and values of the monastic tradition so as to provide a context of meaning for whatever they ask of others. Good example is only one means by which the tradition is passed on; clear thinking and persuasive discourse are also necessary, especially in the early days.

We live in a world in which education systems teach people to question accepted values as a means of finding a path through a pluralistic society. And because knowledge has displaced experience and wisdom as the basic equipment for living, societies in which the young learn from the old are disappearing. In the area of technology, particularly, the young are often summoned to rescue the old from ineptitude. As a result, those entering monasteries and finding there a different way of doing things will want to know why. Because they are generous and good-willed they may accept a facile appeal to convention or tradition once or twice. Eventually, however, they will press for real answers, especially after they have arrived at the relative security of first profession. As Benedict foresaw, those who are in authority over such people will need to have a good understanding of monastic values and the capacity to communicate this wisdom to the next generation. And because many today are disenchanted with authority and preemptively suspicious and fearful of its exercise, first of all authority will have to sell itself before it becomes credible enough to market the tradition it represents.

Monastic teaching is many-layered. There is an important educational component. This involves exposing newcomers to the Scriptures, to the writings of monastic tradition, to theology and history, and to whatever will broaden their minds and further loosen the tightness of their hearts. Ours is a literate tradition, as we have observed in Chapter Four. Even in ruder times monasteries made sure that candidates had acquired basic literacy skill because they had a lifetime of reading ahead of them. Beyond education and study there are many other channels of instruction: the liturgy, for example; the books read in the refectory; sermons or conferences; intelligent discourse within the community. In a particular way seeking and receiving counsel is a fine way of coming to a personal encounter with the tradition and assimilating it in the context of one's own experience. Of course there is always good example, although often this will be a matter of wheat growing among thorns. Most unpopular among the means of formation is the giving of correction. It is this aspect of obedience that we must now consider.

3. Accepting Correction

Benedict prescribes that newcomers are to be taught in advance about all the hard and rough things that will beset their journey to God (58:8). It is impossible, of course, to provide total coverage of hazards that lie in the future. We try to give people a sound basic formation and hope that they will pick up whatever else they need by trial and error. In other words, we expect that they will make just as many mistakes as we did ourselves—and still do.

Experience is a great teacher, but it presupposes a good level of self-awareness. Bernard interprets the text about the just falling seven times in the day as meaning that because they fall during the day they are aware of having fallen, and so can do something about it.[67] That is all very well, but what happens if somebody is not aware of having fallen, or has not perceived the harmful effects that certain actions have on others or may have on themselves in the future?

Augustine notes that appropriate reproof is one of the benefits that we can expect from genuine friendship. If I were engaging in behavior that is liable to be damaging, I would hope that a friend would help me to see the error of my ways. I make mistakes, some of which are unimportant. A few, however, may have results that I would gladly prevent. If somebody else is able to open my eyes to what is going wrong and to encourage me to take contrary action, then I am greatly blessed. If have ongoing access to such a resource, then I can be reasonably relaxed about the choices I make, knowing that if delusion ever gets the better of me, a friend will spot the danger and alert me to it. Correction or putting right is a benefit rather than an added burden.

It often surprises modern readers that Benedict devotes so much space to the question of correction, even to the point of legislating for excommunication for faults. The phrase "regular discipline" is chillingly frequent in the context of any wrongdoing by the monks. Benedict does not allow destructive behavior to go unchecked. Listen to what he says to the abbot: "He is not to pass over the sins of wrongdoers but, as soon as they begin to appear, he is to cut them off at the roots while he is able, mindful of the danger of [sharing the fate of] Eli, the priest of Shiloh" (2:26). Such pastoral interventions are not the expression of a vindictive attitude, nor are they merely punitive in intent. Later chapters reveal that Benedict sees them as stemming from the abbot's compassion for those in trouble, done with the purpose of bringing healing. Indeed he will compare this aspect of the abbot's role to the work of a skilled physician, using all possible means to bring the disaffected brother back to health and wholeness (27:1-2).

Despite Benedict's beautiful image, giving and receiving correction is easy for no one. Monasteries are full of people who are doing their best, and it is not always easy for them to accept a superior's suggestion that something or other needs improvement. In fact such an intervention can sometimes provoke a veritable storm.

> The human heart is like a vessel that may be full either of honey or of poison. For as long as the vessel is closed, nobody knows what is inside. If, however, somebody takes off the lid, then immediately it is possible to smell what is inside. So, brothers, while a monk keeps silence, while nobody says anything to him or tells him to do anything or gives him any occasion to reveal himself, it is as if he were a covered vessel. What is within is not known. But if there is a conversation in which someone commands him to do something that may be burdensome, or if he is corrected for some mistake, then the vessel is uncovered. Then it is possible to detect either a good odor or a bad smell. If he then becomes angry, if he begins to engage in detraction and murmuring, if when there is a possibility he engages in scoffing and mocking and other meaningless behavior, then he is not presenting a good odor to his brothers— since his vessel does not contain fraternal love but a will given to vice.[68]

Aelred seems to be suggesting that it is through the response to correction that we can gauge the depth and quality of a brother's spiritual life. For Aelred the tranquil willingness to accept reproofs is an integral part of the relationship of obedience. He sees it as an essential means of breaking the tyranny of bad habits that are often invisible to ourselves. "Like a sheep, which is an example of simplicity, being neither angry with the shearer nor resistant to its slayer, let him so subject himself simply to the one who corrects him and simply accept the rebuke."[69]

On the other side, giving correction demands discernment and courage, courage because it will almost certainly be unwelcome, discernment because one's own motivation needs to be thoroughly scrutinized. Whether there is scope today for what Clement of Alexandria termed "pedagogical anger" is a question worth pondering. It is probably true that in many places former structures of correction have fallen into disuse, thus placing a greater burden on the initiative of those with pastoral responsibility. Instead of being a routine irritant, correction now usually comes as a shock. Benedict's suggestion that we are more likely to sin by defect than by excess in this matter of pastoral intervention is probably truer in the contemporary world than it ever was. It takes a very special person to be able to accept correction, especially when it is delivered in a manner that is experienced as hurtful. Often, because of the intrinsic difficulty of the situation, there are impedances to clear communication and, as a result, misunderstandings arise that take a lot of good will to resolve. One with pastoral responsibility will have to gauge beforehand whether the risk of intervention is likely to produce a good result; inevitably there will be miscalculations.

Correction is probably one of those situations envisaged by Benedict in the fourth step of humility, where he talks about encountering things that are hard and contrary and meeting with undeserved injuries. His solution is simple though not easy: We embrace Christ's cross. This takes the whole incident from the plane of interpersonal conflict and rancor to a higher and deeper level, where we encounter

Christ, participate in his sufferings and so become more worthy to share in his kingdom.

8 | *Mutuality*

*Let them compete in showing
obedience to one another.*
RB 72:6

St. Benedict's presentation of mutual obedience looks like, and probably was, an afterthought. Having spoken at great length and with strong emphasis about the value of obedience, in the context of the monk's obedience to an abbot, he began to appreciate that the perfect disciple would desire to go further—if he could do so without creating disorder. A monk committed to the practice of mutual obedience is one who has come to the realization that he could be instructed and formed by many members of the community whose monastic experience was broader and deeper than his own. If he remains alert, each day will bring hundreds of opportunities in which he can say "yes" to God and "no" to self-will. If he wanted to, he could turn his whole existence into an orgy of obedience. This ideal and probably nonexistent monk would then begin to look around for other "superiors" from whom he might obtain the benefit of obedience. Progressively he would extend his submission to include not only middle management but also all the petty princelings that monastic life seems to bring into existence. He is voluntarily and uncringingly meek before any who want to give him instructions, be they polite or peremptory.

Needless to say we would want to be sure that such a monk is not just spineless and supine, so uncertain of himself that he needs others to take responsibility for what he does. We would need to be assured that he is not needlessly suppressing his own insights, skills, and talents. We would hope that he is not playing some sort of twisted mind-game whereby he asserts his superiority by a feigned deference or an exaggerated compliance. We return to the question of finality. It is not the submission itself that is praiseworthy but the motivation for which it is embraced, whether this be self-denial, a willingness to learn from others who are smarter and wiser, or a desire to imitate the loving obedience of Christ.

In such a spiritually motivated monk it is probably true to say that generic obedience pre-exists the specific obedience given to those with institutional authority. His "yes" is unconditional precisely because it does not depend on the clout of the one to whom it is given. The phrasing of Benedict's presentation is interesting. "The good of obedience is to be shown by all not only to the abbot, but the brothers are also to obey one another thus, knowing that it is by this road of obedience that they are to go to God" (71:1-2). The Latin seems to imply that it is especially mutual obedience that brings us closer to God. Any who defy institutional authority call down institutional sanctions on their heads; this fear of the negative consequences of disobedience can make our compliance less of an expression of gratuitous love. When we submit to someone of no importance, who has no capacity to penalize our refusal even subtly, then we are deliberately and cold-bloodedly abandoning our own plans and projects in favor of an unnecessary obedience. In a sense this is a purer expression of a desire to abandon self-will, and so a more genuine obedience.

1. The Struggle for Community

Community is a warm and fuzzy term that evokes something deeply satisfying for those of us who have been reared in a world in which individualism is rife. The cry of "Let's build community" was often heard in the 1970s as a protest against forms of religious life that had become over-institutionalized and impersonal. Community and mutuality are certainly attractive ideals, but their practical implementation is neither simple nor easy. It is interesting to note that in the broad range of commentaries that have appeared over the years, few have devoted much attention or manifested much insight on the topic of mutual obedience, whereas vertical obedience has inspired many lyrical pages, especially—as Jean Leclercq once pointed out—by abbots.

Command obedience is easy to understand; the notion of mutual obedience is far more subtle and liable to misinterpretation. It is not some sort of Aquarian democracy. It is not the negation of all management structures or authority. A group in which everybody self-asserts is chaotic to the point of losing all cohesion. In such an unhappy situation, community life becomes the playground of all sorts of sub-personal forces, many of which flourish while their owners are mostly unaware. Conflict and division are the most visible results. As the demise of many experimental communities shows, there need to be formal limits to individualism. Some vertical authority is necessary to ensure that unresolved personal conflicts do not metastasize. The trick is to find a happy medium that goes beyond regimentation and leaves room for personal style and initiative without losing a common sense of purpose in the process.

Lots of people operate reasonably well when they are "in the world" with their own space and a range of safety valves. When they embrace a common life they may find that many of the avenues of recuperation that they hitherto took for granted are unavailable. Pressure builds up, and some of the residue of past history begins to create a ferment inside them. This they attribute to the malign ambiance or the actions of those around them. Before long, instead of reading what is happening inside themselves, they begin to project onto their neighbors the disturbance they feel. Blame takes over: Difference is seen as insensitivity, and everyday thoughtlessness is interpreted as deliberate malice. The ideal of community, so long desired, evaporates before the reality. Mutuality may be an admirable goal but it seems that it cannot be realized in this place, and certainly not with these people.

That this is not a distinctly modern experience is shown from the following quotation from Augustine:

> Here is a man who does not know what goes on inside. He does not know how a wind entering into in a harbor can cause ships to collide. So, he enters the community, hoping for security, and thinking that no one there would need to be tolerated. He finds brothers there who are bad, but who would not have been found to have been bad if they had not been admitted. (It is necessary that first they be tolerated so that maybe they will be corrected; they cannot be easily excluded unless they first be tolerated.) He experiences an impatience that is beyond tolerance. "Who asked me to come here? I was thinking that there was charity here." Thus while he becomes irritated at a few nuisances, he himself does not persevere in the fulfillment of what he vowed. He deserts his holy endeavor and becomes guilty of not rendering what he vowed. And when he departs from that place, he curses it and speaks badly of it. He speaks only of what he endured and insists that he was unable to carry on. Sometimes these [difficulties] are real. However

the real difficulties caused by the evil ought to be tolerated for the sake of association with the good. Scripture says to him, "Woe to those who lose endurance" (Sir. 2:16). Furthermore he belches forth the evil odor of his anger with the result that others about to enter are dissuaded, simply because he himself when he entered was not able to persevere. What are they like in his opinion? They are envious, contentious, non-supportive, mean. This one did such a thing and this other one did that. Wicked man, why are you silent about the good? Why do you speak loudly about those for whom you had no tolerance, and keep quiet about what they had to tolerate because you were bad?[70]

This is where Benedict's insight about mutual obedience is helpful. True community is built on self-denial. If this seems like madness, then understand how necessary it is to rethink basic beliefs and values. I am not saying that mortification is the *purpose* of community life, but it is the *means* by which each person builds up an ambiance of mutuality. I cannot listen if I do not practice restraint of speech. I cannot serve if I seek only to be served or if I am unable to overcome the lazy inertia that renders me motionless. Being attentive to others means becoming forgetful of self. Here, as elsewhere, it is the unconditional character of my benevolence that certifies its integrity. If I think of others only when I feel like it, then my service is no more than an arcane form of self-pleasuring. If my concern is limited to a select few, then it is beginning to look like a form of patronage, and we know how strongly Benedict rejected that (69:1–4). My part in creating a climate of mutuality is to hold back on self-assertion so as to leave room for others. I must be constantly inviting others to flow into the common space, welcoming them, affirming them, even though this has to be done at the price of not asserting my own rights. Where deliberate nonassertion is lacking, real affective community cannot develop.

Of course, I cannot build community on my own, no matter how heroically I give space to others. There is no such thing as unilateral mutuality. The whole point about mutuality is that it is omnidirectional. This implies that I must be not only generous in giving but also gracious in receiving, willing to be loved as much as to love, open to being served as much as outgoing in offering assistance. Those who operate under a compulsion to perform good works need to learn the art of stepping back sometimes and letting others acquire merit. It is only within the context of an integral common life that I can acquire the virtues that are the providential means of my transformation. And it needs to be said that often I acquire these virtues almost unwillingly. They are forced upon me because otherwise my continuing presence in the community would be intolerable both to me and to others. How can I learn patience and forgiveness and the art of saying "Sorry" unless situations arise in which I am called to turn agreeable theory into laborious practice?

The true genius of a genuine monastic community is that it keeps switching roles so that in some situations it is I who am the wrongdoer, in others the victim; in others again, I am both. I have to learn the art of humble apology as well as that of gracious acceptance of apology. In most communities one who presides in one function will be a minor actor or an apprentice in different circumstances. A senior may need to get instructions from a junior, a superior may ask a fraternal favor of a brother, a big man in the community may, in particular circumstances, find himself dependent on a nobody. In one activity I am a parent figure, in another a child. Most of us who live in community take for granted this kind of diverse interaction—but for those who willingly accept such a topsy-turvy approach to status, it is one of the great sources of humility, humanity, and humor. It is one of the reasons for which even famous monastic people are often not so full of themselves or dedicated defenders of their own dignity. Living in a permanent community imparts a quality of groundedness, or even earthiness, that subverts any incipient tendency to self-exaltation.

As with the house at Bethany, many communities will notice divergent tendencies among their members: Some prefer to work, others to entertain. There is no need to view this division of attention adversarially. It is the principle of complementarity of gifts at work. Of course, where there is a latent resentment prowling around looking for someone to devour, difference becomes the target for criticism and disdain. Those more drawn to practical pursuits will be often at war with the spiritually inclined, as Bernard of Clairvaux notes.[71] In a sense, such tension is not only unavoidable but healthy. No single individual possesses all the talents necessary for the realization of a community's corporate potential. Everyone is defective in something. As a result we need one another, and we need to recognize, appreciate, and encourage the different giftedness of others as a means of ensuring the common progress that provides a matrix for my own growth. We are all unavoidably both unique and incomplete. We work best when we work together. Someone with a grand vision will simultaneously be grateful to and irritated by another with the knack of delving into details. As a theoretician I may appreciate the presence of practical people, but this is not to say that cooperating with them is not a challenge.

We can probably take this a step further and say that it is the neediness of the "weak" that encourages the resourcefulness of the "strong." Without the "weak" the "strong" cannot exist. We see this happening in the body: When one system is disabled, another steps in to compensate by taking over some of its functions. For example, those who lose the use of their legs may develop a powerful upper body physique. In the same way, when a family member becomes chronically ill, love impels others to transcend themselves to care for the invalid and to keep the family functioning and together. In a community each member has a particular bundle of strengths and weaknesses. Each contributes not only by being a powerhouse of creative energies, but also by being the end-user of such energies. There is no point in growing parsnips if everybody refuses to eat them. There is no purpose in composing complex troparia if no one will sing them. It is only by responding to the needs of others that we develop our latent gifts. If no need existed then the talents would remain hidden. In this way weakness creates strength. *O wondrous exchange!*

If I accept my limitations and liabilities and look to others to do what I cannot, then we are bound together through many such multi-dimensional interactions. The struggle in building community is often a matter of my not recognizing my need for others. In a sense, it is my failure to see the need to be saved from my own deficiencies, not only by God but by other men and women. Sometimes the best way to turn an enemy into a friend or to restart stalled communications is to ask a favor, to put ourselves in the position of a petitioner, to give the other a chance to demonstrate magnanimity. This is not so easy. Sometimes there will be rebuffs, but the tactic works more often than not, so long as we approach it in a spirit of humility and simplicity. By admitting our "weakness" we allow the other to feel "strong," and most people like us a little more for that.

2. Mutuality and Equality

Benedict's formula for intra-community relationships was, perhaps, modeled on the prescription given to spouses in the Epistle to the Ephesians: "Each of you must love his wife as himself, and the wife should fear the husband" (Eph. 5:33). So towards the end of his list of implements for good work Benedict writes, "Venerate the seniors, love the juniors" (4:70-71 and 63:10). What he means by "venerate" and "honor" is later explained as "obey with all charity and diligence" (71:4). The relationship is not between equals. The honor due to the long monastic experience of the seniors is to be translated into a willingness to learn from them and submit oneself to them. Failure in this matter was interpreted as an expression of contentiousness and stubbornness. As such it was regarded as serious and could lead ultimately to expulsion from the community. Benedict's understanding of "mutual obedience" is not perhaps what we might think the words would indicate.

When it comes to assigning particular functions to the community, Benedict prescribes that the choice is to be guided by the aptitude of the potential appointees, not by their age (63:6) or, surprisingly, by their rank (*ordo*) in the community, otherwise a significant element for Benedict in determining community relations. Abbots and deans are to be chosen "according to their meritorious life and wise doctrine and not *per ordinem*" (21:4), "even though the last *in ordine* of the community" (64:2). Singers and readers are nominated "according to their capacity to edify the hearers and not *per ordinem*" (38:12). As brothers all are equal, but the capacity of each for particular tasks is unequal. It is the abbot's task to discern the particular gifts of those he governs and to assign to each roles and functions that will enable them to do what they are given with facility and flair.

From what has been said, community life as shaped by mutual obedience is not a matter of perfect homogeneity. Quite the contrary! All are equal in their dependence on others, and in honoring their duty to mutual service (35:1), but the shape of each relationship is fluid and uneven. Mutual obedience is not collegiality, in which all have equal status and authority. In most cases mutuality does not deprive superiors of their right to give orders, as

Benedict states explicitly (71:3). Those who are in charge of departments are still in charge. Even in the process of consultation, there is complementarity rather than equality between giving counsel and receiving it.

> I believe that "the good zeal that monks ought to have" (RB 72) is to be exercised always in a community of unequals, a community of the weak and the strong, of some with one gift and others another, of those who need more and those who need less, of the advanced and less advanced in the monastic way of life. All are radically one in Christ (2:20), all are brothers to one another within the community. Yet the community is complex, messy, diverse. Each member has a specific place within it. Relationships are not perfectly symmetrical. There is nothing smoothly egalitarian about it at all. It is in such a community of unequals that the brothers are called to practise obedience with the warmest love (72:3).[72]

People have different gifts and different areas of skill and expertise. This inequality is grounded in reality rather than in privilege, although it may happen that at different stages of a community's history some talents will be more highly prized and praised than others. True mutuality is based on recognition of the intrinsic dignity of each person rather than on their extrinsic status or position. Native giftedness is one source of differentiation; on the other hand, as Benedict recognizes many, many times throughout the course of the Rule, particular individuals often have special needs. "[The abbot] should have an equal love for all and for all maintain a single discipline according to their merits" (2:22). Charity is universal, but the application of the rule needs to accommodate the particularities of individuals. "Let [the abbot] know what a difficult and arduous task it is to govern souls and to be at the service of many [different] dispositions" (2:31). This delicacy is evident in the statement of principle that Benedict often uses to open his chapters. "Every age and intelligence has a distinctive measure" (30:1). "Distribution was made as each had need" (34:1). "Although human nature is drawn to mercy in dealing with old men and children, nevertheless the authority of the rule must also make provision for them" (37:1). "Each has his own gift from God, one this and another that" (40:1). Action based exclusively on the principle of equality is often very unfair; it penalizes some and gives others an easy time. This is why Benedict so often advocates differentiation according to individual qualities and moderation. In this way everything is done according to due measure, some receiving more, others less. "Let [the abbot] temper all things so that the strong will have what they desire and the weak will not seek refuge [elsewhere]" (64:19).

Because all are different each is called to curtail private preferences so as to make room for others in the common space. This self-denial is relatively easy when it results in a visible benefit to another, especially if that other is cherished. It is a bit harder when it means submitting to a numerical majority or *force majeure*. The ability to give way to an extrinsic will is even more necessary when it comes to accepting the "common will" of the community. In his younger days Thomas Merton developed a strong theory about this, developing an idea he picked up from Bernard, though somewhat beyond its original intent.[73] Living in community involves my recognizing that I am not alone in the house. I do not have unrestricted access to community resources—these are to be shared by all. I alone do not have the right to decide future directions; each accredited member will have something to contribute to the common vision. If something is to be done, all are to be consulted, and sometimes the solution adopted will go against my preferences. I need to have an entrenched belief in the probable integrity of options taken as a result of the common decision-taking and leave the outcome to Providence. For me to isolate myself from a community activity because I disagree with aspects of policy is destructive both of community harmony and of my own progress. If I have painted myself into a corner by being too dogmatic and outspoken, I may end up very lonely. We saw examples of this in the years following the Second Vatican Council; those unwilling to accept the common will regarding particular adaptations withdrew into their own world of indignant righteousness, denying to themselves the benefit of fraternity and the possibility of future influence, and depriving the community of the blessing of loyal opposition.

Participation is an essential component of effective community; without it morale declines, tasks are less efficiently performed, and the quality of relationships is degraded. Before any participation occurs, however, there must be a willingness to participate, to take part in community activities and discussions. Taking part means exactly what it says: taking a *part* of the action—not nothing and not the whole. It means being involved in a corporate enterprise, claiming for oneself no more than a measure of the totality. Let me exaggerate the mathematics of this for a moment. If I am one of a community of twenty, I am justly expected to contribute about one-twentieth of its exertions, and I have the right to no more than one-twentieth of its resources. I participate appropriately in a community discussion by speaking for one-twentieth of the time and by listening to nineteen-twentieths of the time. Beyond that rough proportion, there is a possibility that I am restricting my participation to its active mode and forgetting to leave scope for others. It is not always easy to know when to act and when to stay still, when to speak and when to listen, especially when matters concern me directly. Knowing when will be easier if we really want to do the right thing and if we recognize that, more often than not, doing the right thing is a matter of negating the impulses of self-will.

This is not the place to repeat what I have written elsewhere concerning the bane of individuality or, as it was termed in the monastic Middle Ages, "singularity."[74] Western culture is profoundly individualistic, and this makes community living unnecessarily difficult. Most of us enter the monastery with a deep-seated conviction that we have the right to run our own lives any way we want to, and it is not incumbent on anybody else to tell us how we should act, what we should wear or when we should do something. We prefer to think that we reserve such decisions to ourselves. If we were living on our own, such an attitude would not matter much. In community we need to change, to break down the defensive barriers and let other people into our life—not just one or two whom we happen to like, but people in general. This means that we offer hospitality to all, permitting them to enter our lives, to look around and make comments. And we are not afraid to listen to them and pay attention. They may be donkeys, but sometimes they utter oracles that come from God. On the other hand we are prepared to accept the invitation of others to come closer, knowing as we do, that opening the frontiers will inevitably make demands on us.

There is an ascetical character in mutuality, because it is one of the most effective means of combating unrestrained self-will. It would, however, be misleading to see mutual obedience merely as mortification. Its function goes beyond that because it lays a very solid foundation on which affective community can be built.

3. From Empathy to Intimacy

In the Acts of the Apostles the common life of the primitive community seems to derive from the fact that they had but one heart and one soul. For most of us, the dynamic probably goes in the opposite direction. It is through years of living together and sharing first tasks and then vision, that affective bonds are formed and strengthened. When we enter a community our contact with most other members is superficial and usually lopsided. We probably had not previously encountered them in their home environment and seen them acting as themselves. We may have tried to project onto them all sorts of false ideals and then were disappointed that they failed to live up to them.

The price of seeing others as they really are is to stop play-acting and to allow others to see us as we are, without pretense or self-inflation and not trying to disguise our limitations or defects. Self-knowledge is, as Bernard often insisted, the basis of all compassion—which was the word that he used for what we would call empathy. If I accept myself then I am far less likely to be dismayed by the folly of others and far more likely simply to welcome them as they are. All true friendship is conditional on the truth of my perception of my friends. I cannot really be a friend to someone I idealize. I may be an admirer or a fan, but I cannot be a friend. In this situation probably there is much in the other which I do not accept simply because I cannot perceive it. Friendship means understanding how another's virtues interact with vices, how melancholy may follow moments of high humor, and creativity may give way to listless inertia. A friend is a "man for all seasons," and there is no better way of seeing persons in all their seasonal variation than living in community with them, sharing their ups and downs. Those whom we meet only when both of us feel like it can be enjoyable companions, but we don't have to deal with each other when one or both is in a bad mood. In community there is no escape from the whole truth, and because of this there is the possibility that all our relationships, some deeper than others, will be more truthful.

To the extent that we are self-aware we will probably tend to grow in understanding of others. Our own experience opens the door to feelings of solidarity. My personal experience is as a man in a community of men. I have the impression that there is much in the dynamics of affective community that is gender-specific. It seems that pure empathy comes more naturally to women than to men.[75] Men seem to concentrate on getting systems in operation, uniting to complete a project, and finding friendship in shared endeavor. Ask us to sit around and relate and most would be at a loss. I suppose that it does not much matter at which end of the continuum we begin, building community presupposes both affective love and effective love: feelings of communion and the capacity to share one another's lives, on the one hand, and, on the other, the willingness to unite in pursuing a common goal, whether this be an ultimate ideal or merely the efficient completion of a practical project.

How is it possible to create a community dynamic that is omnidirectional without being chaotic? Probably the best foundation is the acceptance of a common discipline of life, *conversatio*, motivated by a shared fund of beliefs and values, and powered by a single finality, the search for union with God. But that is only the foundation. Effective community is but a first step in the direction of affective community. Those who are of one mind in their pursuit of the monastic ideal soon find themselves growing in affection for one another so that they also find themselves becoming more and more of one heart. Thus the community becomes, slowly but surely, a school of love. In our times, when the incidence of family fragmentation is increasing, many men and women who enter monasteries bear serious affective wounds, and some may even be hoping to avoid the traumas that love seems to inflict. Unconsciously they are looking for love, yet they are fearful of intimacy. For such people an authentic and loving community may represent affective redemption. The experience of a love that is not poisoned by violence or exploitation gradually helps to restore their humanity, and is the necessary condition for their growth in holiness.

The key component of such nurturing is trust. These days, in which the Church and many of its instrumentalities no longer enjoy the routine trust once given it by its members, we have to work hard to win the confidence of those who come to us. We have to survive a twenty-four-hour scrutiny in which will be weighed our honesty and integrity, our clarity of vision together with our competence in implementing it in practice, and, on an interpersonal level, our approachability, affability, and capacity for two-way communication. Only if we have attained an acceptable level in all these areas will trust be forthcoming. We have to *earn* trust, and it seems that the only way that we can do this, especially if we are in the front line of formation, is to live at a level of fervor much higher than that with which we would otherwise be content.

The presence of new life in the community in the form of a new generation of recruits, is a general invitation to greater fidelity. By being what we are called to be, we give newcomers an inkling of what they can become if they continue to pursue the monastic ideal. This modeling is an arduous responsibility—but there are benefits for us as well. We re-discover our own ideals in the aspirations of the young and—if we allow it to happen—we are spurred on by their enthusiasm. This is true mutuality, where each finds in the other the means of growth and fervor.

The interchange that trust facilitates is not merely at the level of interpersonal relationships. It also allows for deeper communion at the level of faith and charism, in which the handing on of the tradition becomes inseparable from sensitivity to the signs of the times. This harmony between generations, in which each keeps its special characteristic, is surely what Benedict intended when he recommended respecting the seniors and loving the juniors. There is no place for polarization or class struggle, but the blending together of linked but opposite energies for renewal.

Benedictine peace is the result of walking on two legs instead of trying to hop ahead on one.

Such trust renders competitiveness unlikely and makes it possible for me to cling less tenaciously to what is (perhaps temporarily) mine. By this means I become willing to add my resources and gifts to the common pool so that what I am and what I have are at the service of communion and not merely elements in a program of self-enhancement. Baldwin of Forde spoke eloquently about this in his tractate *On the Common Life.*

> [Charity] loves to have things in common, not to possess them individually without sharing them. In fact, it loves to share them so much that it is sometimes unwilling to reclaim good which rightfully belong to it and which someone else has taken. Charity is generous and shuns disputes; it does not seek its own interests and has no wish to enter into legal controversy, when charity itself would be in danger. It prefers to be cheated than to perish; to suffer the damages rather than be awarded the costs. Why would it be eager to reclaim what it does not have? Individual gifts are led by [charity] to [serve] the common good, and a gift which one person has received as his own personal possession becomes of benefit to another because its usefulness is shared with him. . . . Someone who has should share with those who have not, as we are taught by him who says, "Give, and it shall be given to you.". . . Thus, whoever is good to himself should also be good to others and not troublesome. Whoever has the utterance of wisdom or knowledge, whoever has the gift of work or service, whoever has any other gift, whether greater or lesser, should possess it as having been given by God for the

sake of others. He should always be afraid that
a gift he has received may turn against him if he
does not strive to use it for the benefit of others,
for we receive the gift of God in vain if we do not
use it to seek the glory of God and the benefit
of our neighbor. But if the personal gift which
some[one has received] from God is turned to the
common good, it is then that this gift is changed
into the glory of God, and when the gift given
to each one individually is possessed in common
through the sharing of love, then the fellowship
of the Holy Spirit is truly with us.[76]

Monastic community and mutuality are realized most
fully in the communion of adult disciples gathered around
God's Word, looking forward to the coming of the kingdom.
Preferring nothing to Christ's love, each gives priority to
another, and all bear one another's burdens. Oddly enough
such concern for others does not issue in the annihilation
of self but makes way for its flowering. True community is
the matrix of both originality and creativity.

9 | *Generativity*

> *Let him be as a father to the*
> *whole community.*
> RB 31:2

One of the problems with responding to the individual neediness of the "weak" is that it can lead to neglect of the "strong." They are considered to have no need of encouragement and support. All are easily convinced that those with abundant gifts can look after themselves. Many people find it fulfilling to be a source of comfort and strength to those in trouble and so, unconsciously, they tend to reward those who seek this kind of care from them, and thereby give the message that neediness is the most effective way of getting attention and love. There is danger here of setting up a co-dependency situation in which neither party grows toward a more mature autonomy. At the level of community, priority given to the "weak" may force those who are "strong" either to deny their strength so as to be eligible for pastoral concern, or to develop their gifts in isolation from the community. In either case the community loses out. As Ayn Rand demonstrated in her novel *Atlas Shrugged*, rewarding weakness and penalizing strength is a surefire recipe for social decline.

An effective community needs every single member to be operating at the peak of their present potential—at least, most of the time. No doubt this introduces wild cards into the community dynamic—control freaks will certainly feel uneasy at the prospect. A community that defines its activities as much by the talents of its members as by precedent or market forces will certainly need a large measure of courage and a good capacity for discernment and dialogue. Nobody quite knows what previously undiscovered gifts will emerge as a person develops, but there is no need to be afraid. We have all been acquainted with monks and nuns who have been ordinary enough people at the beginning of their monastic life and who, at some point down the track, began to blossom. In the right circumstances during mid-life we often see an explosion of talents that we never expected: Music, art, or some useful craft, writing or teaching, a knack for administration, an empathy that heals others' wounds, an affability that creates common warmth, a wisdom that forms and nourishes. These are community-building gifts. By their means a community thrives; without them we will be condemned to a sterile, precedent-bound mediocrity.

In celibate communities attention must be paid to encouraging generativity. This means that it is not only those in leadership positions who are seen as responsible for expressing the charism and transmitting it to the next generation, but each person in the community. This is probably why we see Benedict modifying the autocratic abbacy envisaged by *The Rule of the Master* and making provision for the abbot's ministry to be complemented by that of deans, the prior, the senior in charge of novices, the cellarer and "the spiritual seniors" who act where he cannot.

1. A Generative Community

In some avian species the paramount leader, the alpha male, is distinguished by its brightly-colored plumage and by its appropriation of all the females in the group, thus ensuring total paternity of the next generation. This is not the ideal that Benedict envisages for the leader of the monastic flock. The arduous task of leadership is not about the abbot, but about those whom he is appointed to serve. His task is to be of use to them rather than to claim privileges for himself: *prodesse magis quam praeesse* (64:8). *Auctoritas*, deriving from the verb *augere*, is named for its task of facilitating growth. Benedict's abbot is not intended as a fine-feathered father of the next generation, but as one who encourages a wider flowering of generativity, in the officials, the deans, and the spiritual seniors, and through them in the whole community. In the text that stands at the head of this chapter, the abbot is instructed to share his paternity with officials in the community—in this case the cellarer. It is a principle that has a great importance in preparing for the future of the community. Beyond the simple vertical relationship of father and son, master and disciple, teacher and student, there are other relationships in a community that facilitate growth in the upcoming generation. These are specific examples of that general mutuality which is typical of a dynamic community. They are instances of the "horizontal relations" noted as a characteristic of Benedict's Rule.[77]

Just as mutuality is not to be equated with equality, so generativity exists in more than one mode. Generativity takes a variety of forms, each with its own nuance. There is, for example, an important distinction that needs to be made between mentoring and nurturing. Mentors can play a significant role in the transition to full adult maturity by accepting younger colleagues as apprentices and bringing them to a level of equality. There can be an implicit expectation that the younger person will not surpass the older, nor deviate too radically from the parameters the mentor has accepted. To breach these boundaries often leads to a painful rupture of the relationship. Nobody likes to be surpassed by one who, only yesterday, was a beginner.[78] Perhaps hidden in the mentoring relationship is an element of co-dependency: one needing to exercise control and the other welcoming it. This is an imperfect generativity in so far as it often consists in remaking another person in one's own image and likeness rather than sowing a seed and allowing it to grow to its own limits.

Necessary mentorship has a limited life and, if it is faithful to its purpose, must come to an end. Nurturing, however, because it is a purer function of love, goes on forever. Handing on a tradition in a way that transcends one's own embodiment of it is a very self-sacrificing task that necessarily involves a renunciation of control. It involves not only bringing others to a par with myself, but encouraging them to surpass me, to become better than I in doing what I do well. Nurturance is a road to redundancy. Far from being a way to create a personal empire, it is the willingness to step aside so that others may develop their talents and help to redefine the community's future in a manner that goes beyond my particular vision.

Making provision for a broader generativity in monasteries seems to me one of the urgent issues that needs to be confronted creatively. I am not alone in this belief. This is what Abbot General Bernardo Olivera writes on the topic as it applies in monasteries of the Cistercian Strict Observance.

> As we all know, the kinds of service that allow one to feel like a "leading actor" in some area are few in the monastery: the abbot or abbess, novice director, cellarer, cantor or chantress . . . This means that many monks and nuns of generative age

find no place to channel their potential, which may lead to a sense of frustration affecting themselves and others. We might make a distinction here according to gender, even though not everyone will accept it. In nuns' monasteries, it would appear that the generative capacity is the exclusive domain of the Mother Abbess, or, by remote extension, of another sister in her immediate orbit. In monks' monasteries, other fathers (with a lower case "f") are allowed, even though there is only one Father Abbot. . . . To put it more concretely, there is not always sufficient room or outlet for the generative capacity proper to adult professed monks and nuns, understood in general terms as the role of affirming and orienting the following generation. Not uncommonly, this is a source of crises and setback on the way to human and spiritual maturity. Even celibacy and virginity for the sake of the Kingdom can end up being lived out in a castrating way. Frustrated generativity causes withdrawal into oneself, obsessive search for intimacy, invalidity at an early age, excessive worry about oneself. On the contrary, a positive living-out of generativity opens horizons, provides mutual enrichment, increases vital human energy, all of which brings with it an appetite for living.[79]

Part of the problem of a lack of generativity is its invisibility. The abuses to which it leads can be seen and deplored, but sterility itself cannot be directly perceived. Who knows whether an external quiescence is not the counterpart of a hidden interior fruitfulness? Or whether the tree is merely wintering or in an irreversible march towards death? The voices of the ungenerative are rarely heard; they tend not to participate in meetings and chapters. They are often regarded as a dead weight that retards the progress of "the community." Even though they are less interesting people to deal with than the talented and enthusiastic, perhaps these dying branches should become a significant focus of pastoral zeal, not merely to comfort and console them, but to challenge them to put forth buds, to flower and yield fruit. It is not merely a question of palliative care but of summoning into life the latent gifts that have long lain dormant. The abbot "should be aware that he has undertaken the care of weak souls and not a reign of terror (*tyrannidem*) over the healthy" (27:6). Bernard of Clairvaux develops this thought in one of his letters, written to a former disciple who had himself become an abbot.

> Souls are the burden we carry—weak souls. Those who are healthy do not need to be carried and so they are not a burden. But when you find any of yours who are sad, fearful or grumbling know that it is of these that you are the father, of these you are abbot. By advising, exhorting and rebuking, you do your job, you carry your burden, for it is by carrying that you heal those whom you carry. . . . Knowing that you have been sent to help and not to be helped, understand that you are there as the representative of him who came to serve and not be served.[80]

Superiors who are anxious to cultivate, maintain, and secure their own generativity may easily forget their crucial role of acting as a catalyst for the creativity of others. This omission can have serious negative effects in the long term. What is encouraged is more easily guided and kept within community parameters, whereas what arises in the teeth of opposition or indifference is often a wild growth that may, in the last analysis, deny any benefit to the community and contribute little to the general vitality.

It is important to insist that this pastoral care is more than keeping people calm and apparently happy—drugged to the eyebrows with superficial solace and sympathy. Sometimes genuine concern involves upsetting their peaceful existence; urging them to break out of the cast-iron frameworks in which their lives are lived, to take risks, to cast their nets in deeper waters. This might mean, in the first place, withdrawing the occasions for self-medication by escapist hobbies, entertainments, and substance abuse, and then giving them jobs beyond what they believe they can manage, supporting them as they struggle to acquire new skills and patiently feeding back to them the elements of a new self-image.

There is a further complication. Fostering creativity needs to be universal. Selective facilitation of generativity may be little more than the favoritism that Benedict rejects (2:16, 2:20, 34:2). It is easy to encourage those who are responsive to our interventions and who are willing to accept our patronage (69:1). It is a much more demanding to recognize the gifts of those who are churlish or somewhat hostile, to cherish them and to provide possibilities for their development. The task of generating generators often demands a good measure of self-forgetfulness.

A final cautionary note: In encouraging others to use their talents discretion is always necessary. Benedict recognizes that the primacy of monastic *conversatio* must never be displaced by the exercise of particular talents or skills (57:1-2). It is particularly important to remember this today, when many communities have large gaps in their middle ranks. Prematurely placing competent young persons in positions of responsibility may inhibit their monastic formation, prevent their normal growth into the fabric of a particular community, and even be a threat to their perseverance. In the early years of formation, of course, it is forbidden by canon law as well as by common sense. But sometimes local urgencies seem to overrule both. As with everything else, there is a time to receive and be formed and a time to be generative. Mostly the period of generativity coincides with mid-life and beyond—it builds on the foundation of the formative experience of growing into monastic life and slowly being imprinted with the character of the particular community. These are slow processes that cannot prudently be hurried in order to cater to external demands.

2. Monastic Subculture

One of the fringe benefits of monastic community is that it encourages a certain refinement in those who are attuned to its subtle rhythms. In interaction there is an expectation of civility and politeness, even a little formality. Sensitivity to others, thoughtfulness, and good manners are viewed as concrete means of expressing and reinforcing charity. Scurrility and obstreperous behavior are ideally excluded. The roughest of diamonds cannot avoid acquiring some degree of polish if they last long in a monastery. There are, of course, blatant exceptions to this rule.

Monastic life, as we have seen, stretches one's intellectual boundaries by its insistence on wide and regular reading. It expects of all a certain finesse in liturgical participation and, generally, tries to cultivate good taste in music and aesthetic appreciation. It is possible that this sophistication is no more than an elegant patina adopted to disguise an empty life. Most often it is not. There is a change in personal style as monastic life takes hold of one. In entering a monastery we move into a different world with its own subculture.[81]

We should not think, however, that the monastic subculture is just a matter of conversion of manners. It goes deeper than that. The external forms that express the distinctiveness of monastic living have an important function in conserving and transmitting the values they embody. Domestic rituals and local customs are important for groups—they provide insulation for the group's particular values, they support identity, and they play a positive role in the development of good morale and esprit de corps. Common activities do more than merely sustain individuals while the process of internalizing values continues; they also express in a wordless way some of the priorities by which a community lives. Formation of newcomers is more than accompanying them while some inner seed comes to maturity: There needs to be an active interchange of elements between the community and the individual, a fusion of horizons. Nor can the communication of a charism take place only by teaching and dialogue: Participation in the practicalities of community life is essential, whereby the powerful magic of good example provides models according to which newcomers can re-imagine their own future and so grow into something different.

There are three stages in the emergence of generativity. The first is when a person becomes *productive*, joining in the work of the group and filling a slot in its assembly line— achieving an acceptable result that approximates the norm. This may be followed by varying degrees of *being creative*, in which the work done is more or less enhanced by individual flair. Instead of just delivering a product, the doer of the task accomplishes some level of self-expression. This addition, which is deeply satisfying to the one responsible, need not be intrusive or offensive to others. Think of an organist who passes beyond competence to a level of expertise that pleases everyone, or a cook who transforms monastic meals from merely edible to delicious.[82] This middle phase can be a source of great joy to all in so far as the "self" that is expressed is not the chaotic and individualistic self of everyday experience but the "deeper self" that comes to the surface only through years of ascetical practice. It is, however, self-denial in the form of self-transcendence, that leads to the final stage. *Generativity* is not a riot of individualistic self-expression, but a stepping aside so that the charism and the tradition that I have internalized may find expression through what I do. True generativity is a matter of transmitting the life I have received and made my own to the next generation. What I give is something truly my own, and yet it is larger than I. The one who receives it from me receives it whole and will translate it into forms that are beyond my imagining. The gift I received, I have passed on. I cannot control what it will become. This is the mystery of tradition—the hidden transmission of life to the next generation. True generativity is not the exaltation of the ego but its deference to the contagious energy of a charism that leaps from one person to another in ways often concealed from the participants.

The continuance of the monastic charism is one of the prime functions of a monastic community; that is why when there is no one to receive the gift communities often lose vitality to the point of seeming dead, even though the previous generation is still officially surviving. Handing on the charism is not an optional extra, reserved perhaps to some formally designated functionaries. It is an *essential*, though not necessarily self-conscious, part of living the charism. The more the members of a community become aware of their responsibility to hand on to the next generation what has been received from the past, the more effectively formative the community is. A community is fully alive when all its members continually receive the tradition into themselves, appropriate it interiorly, and then, in a harmonious way, express it exteriorly through their actions so that it becomes communicable to others. It is by this recycling succession of moments that a monastic culture is generated.

The most visible aspects of culture are its artifacts. We who live in a consumer society are beginning to forget what it is like to make things: to define a need, to design a process or a product that will meet that need, and then to create a suitable object. If we need something we go to a shop and buy it. Most of us would be completely lost if we were marooned on a desert island or forced to survive the destruction of urban civilization. We would not have a clue about what to do once our credit cards stopped providing us with the necessities of life. One of the aspects of medieval monasteries that fascinates me is the ingenuity exercised by monks and lay brothers in working things out, harnessing nature, inventing gadgets, and developing skills to make life livable. I am always delighted when I find a similar attitude to life in modern monasteries—perhaps it happens only when money is short and time is ample. But maybe something else is needed: a mind that sees problems, asks questions, and is not afraid to seek solutions. How good it is to see people applying themselves to practical problems and using head and hands to fix it. A monastery becomes a very special place when many of the objects one sees around or handles in daily use are of local design or manufacture. This is a basic level of objective culture. Arts and crafts also add something to the common life, although they demand more specialized skills. The fact that the products are "homemade" should be considered a benefit that ought not to be sacrificed at the altar of globalized slickness. There are more important issues at stake than keeping up with the Joneses.

Whether it is a question of bread, rosary beads, or perfume, objects that have been produced in monasteries are often regarded as special because of the manner in which they are made. Monastic men and women are presumed to have a passion for excellence, good taste, and a non-exploitative attitude. Between ourselves, this is not always the case. There are also monastic hucksters who are out for every cent they can squeeze out of the market, but let us pretend that these are the exceptions. Such romantic expectations are, however, good reminders of how we ought to act when we do what we do, whether it is bookbinding, cheese-making, teaching, writing, or serving a liturgical function. The ideal is that monastic workers are not mindless robots but fully engaged persons who leave the imprint of what they are on what they produce, whether it be for internal consumption or for sale. Their work is not merely a necessary occupation or a hobby, but something that flows directly from the center of their being.

Objective culture is the outcome of subjective culture. That is to say that all the various components of a culture have their origin in fully alive human beings. The more vital the generators of culture, the livelier the fruits of their efforts. Following in the wake of the Vatican II decree *On the Church in the Modern World* that identified culture as one of five key areas of concern, Pope John Paul II has often emphasized this humanizing aspect of cultural dynamism: "Culture is that by which man as man becomes more man."[83]

> The experience of the various eras, without excluding the present one, proves that people think of culture and speak about it *in the first place in relation to the nature of [the human being], then only in a secondary and indirect way in relation to the world of products.*[84]

> There is no doubt that the first and fundamental cultural fact is the spiritually mature [human being], that is a fully educated [human being], one capable of educating himself and educating others.[85]

> True culture is humanization, whereas non-culture and false cultures are dehumanizing. For this reason, in the choice of culture it is [human] destiny which is at stake. Humanization, namely [human] development, is carried out in all fields of reality in which [human beings] are situated and take their place: in their spirituality or corporeity,

in the universe, in human and divine society. It is
a question of a harmonious development, in which
all the sectors to which human beings belong are
connected with one another. . . . Culture must
cultivate human beings and all human beings in
the extension of an integral and full humanism,
in which the whole human being and all human
beings are helped to advance in the fullness of
every human dimension. Culture has the essential
purpose of bettering human beings and procuring
for all the goods necessary for the development of
their individual and social being.[86]

These quotations and many others like them demonstrate
the linkage existing between moral and spiritual development,
becoming ever more human, and the generation of culture. A
monastery that exists for the purposes of spiritual growth will
necessarily promote human development and, thereby, create
an ambiance favorable to the emergence, maintenance, and
expansion of culture. It will be a place of generativity.

3. Utopia?

Sometimes it seems that the monastic microcosm could
easily become a realization of the utopian dream of
which many great thinkers have written. Indeed, some of
the medieval portrayals of monasteries such as Clairvaux
tend in this direction. The first description comes from
William, a friend of Bernard, who had been abbot of the
Benedictine monastery of Saint-Thierry and later became
a Cistercian monk of Signy. Needless to say, he describes
Clairvaux in terms of his own imagined ideals: poverty,
solitude, order, and harmony.

At that time [it was a sight for sore eyes] to see Clairvaux in its golden age. Men of virtues who had previously been rich and honored in the world now glory in Christ's poverty. They planted God's church in their own blood, in labor and in troubles, in hunger and thirst, in cold and nakedness, in persecutions, insults and under many constraints and thus prepared for Clairvaux the sufficiency and peace which it has today. They considered that they lived not for themselves but for Christ and for the brothers who would serve God in that place. They dismissed as nothing what they themselves lacked and, mindful of the voluntary poverty [they had undertaken] for Christ's sake, they sought only to leave behind them what would suffice to meet the necessities [of those that followed].

Coming down the mountain those arriving had their first view of Clairvaux. Through the simplicity and humility of the building the mute valley spoke of the simplicity and humility of the poor of Christ who lived there. The valley was full of people. No one was idle but everyone was at work, each at the task enjoined him. Even at midday those arriving would find a silence like that of midnight, except for the sound of work or if the brothers were engaged in the praise of God. This rule of silence and their high reputation engendered a sense of reverence even among lay people who arrived so that they were fearful of speaking there, not only about obscene or idle matters but of anything that was not necessary.

The place itself in which the servants of God hid themselves was solitary, surrounded by thick forests and constrained within the sides of nearby mountains. It somehow recalled the cave in which our holy father Benedict was found by shepherds. So as they imitated his life and house, these men would also appear to have some form of his solitude.

All the multitude in that place were solitaries. Although the valley was full of people their ordered charity, because it was ordered by reason, made them all solitary. A single disorderly person can become as a crowd, even when alone. In that place, where there was unity of spirit and a regular law of silence, this ordered lifestyle guarded the solitude of heart for each member of that well-ordered multitude of people.[87]

Fifty years later an anonymous author gives a picture of Clairvaux in all its serene glory. He emphasizes the great variety of works undertaken by the monks in clearing the land and in planting crops, vineyards, orchards, and gardens where the sick may sit to be serenaded by the birds. Then he traces the course of the river Aube as it winds through the monastery "not by nature but thanks to the industry of the brothers." It visits all the workshops in turn, bestowing its blessing on each: the gardens, the fish farm, the mill, the workshop of the fullers, the tannery, the kitchen, and, finally, the latrines. Then it continues on its way through grassy meadows.

This place is beautiful with much that relieves weary minds, dissolves anxiety and grief and greatly inflames the devotion of those who seek the Lord, and turns their minds to heavenly delight for which we long. The smiling face of earth with all its many colors feeds the eyes with its aspect of spring and breathes pleasant fragrance into the nose.[88]

Going beyond topographical beauty and ordered industry, Bernard of Clairvaux continues the theme of the cloistral paradise, but his perspective concentrates on a unity that derives not from uniformity or regimentation but from harmonious variety.

> The monastery is truly a paradise, a region fortified with the rampart of discipline. It is a glorious thing to have men living together in the same house, following the same way of life. How good and pleasant it is when brothers live in unity. You will see one of them weeping for his sins, another rejoicing in the praise of God, another tending the needs of all, and another giving instruction to the rest. Here is one who is at prayer, another at reading. Here is one who is compassionate and another who inflicts penalties for sins. This one is aflame with love and that one is valiant in humility. This one remains humble when everything goes well and the other one does not lose his nerve in difficulties. This one works very hard in active tasks while the other finds quiet in the practice of contemplation.[89]

Many secular descriptions of Utopia seem totalitarian in concept, derived from a particular philosophy which is then imposed on all. We need to remember that they are fictional.[90] It is probably not possible to create a perfect human society without paying serious attention to the reality of sin and, therefore, without having inbuilt access to the remedy for sin: the grace of God. Dr. Peter Cock, an Australian sociologist who founded the Moora Moora community in 1974, wrote thirteen years later, "If I were doing it again, I'd set up a religious community."[91]

A monastic community becomes a heaven not because its theory and structures are correct and its personnel are perfect, but because it is a zone of mercy. In Bernard's view, spiritual life begins with self-knowledge, progresses via compassion or empathy, and finds its completion in the self-forgetfulness of contemplation. In such a culture perceived imperfections are not denied or papered over but are reframed by reference to a God who forgives and draws all into reconciliation.

A monastery that follows the Rule of Benedict aims to become a moral rather than a political Utopia because all those who live there strive to become fully alive human beings in a situation that draws the best from them. This does not mean that all are always strong or talented in every pursuit. Instead this ideal community calls forth a cheerful complementarity of strong and weak, young and old, outstanding and average. The gifts of one complete those of another and belong to all. It is not merely a matter of having perfect structures; it is the quality of those who live in monasteries that creates a cloistral paradise, a reflection of heaven on earth.

Before I am howled down by those who consider monastic community closer to purgatory than to heaven, let me add a qualification. The cloistral paradise is still in the stage of becoming. But it is conformity to the image of heaven that is the goal of the community's corporate journey. But, as we have mentioned, the primary characteristic both of the ultimate expression of the ideal and its imperfect realization here on earth is mercy. An earthly community approaches perfection in so far as it is a living expression of mercy, forgiveness, toleration, compassion, reconciliation. To implement these qualities there must be those who need to be endured, tolerated, forgiven, and reconciled. By the grace of God our communities abound in such persons. Without them we would have no hope of becoming more heavenlike. How the angels must giggle at our self-righteous condemnation of such trivial offenders! Far from being obstacles in our path, those whose perfection is less evident are an integral part of God's scheme to transform us into total likenesses to Christ.

The rebirth of monastic tradition in each successive generation is possible only when those who have received the charism are willing to let go of it in order to pass it one to others. This can happen unconsciously, but it is much better when members of the community are fully aware both of the challenge and the call to be bearers of light and life to those who come after them—both by receiving and giving, by doing and being done. This gives a purpose in life, a sense of fulfillment that enables us to leap over the minor idiocies with which our path is littered, and to hasten with sober speed towards the goal of all our endeavors.

10 | *Christist*

> *To put nothing before the love of Christ*
> RB 4:21

We have to be careful in speaking about the monastic charism. There is a danger that we objectify it to the extent that it becomes a commodity rather than a relationship. In fact, the heart of all monastic observance is communion with Christ realized in prayer, in love for the brothers and sisters, and in the sacramental overlap of these relationships in the liturgy. Christian monasticism is not a system of spiritual self-improvement; it is a means that some people need to sustain and deepen their relationship to Christ. Everything else is secondary to that goal.

Christianity defines self-realization in terms of relationship with God. We also affirm that the "way" or "road" by which human fulfillment is obtained is a dynamic and deepening personal relationship to Jesus. Juridicizing theology has been able to void this distinctive imperative by making salvation a matter of some objective work that Jesus did on our behalf ("redemption" which supplies us with "grace") or, alternatively, the effect of our moral adherence to what Jesus did and taught. Any system of spirituality based on such extrinsic benefits is superficial and unable to sustain life in hard times. Christian religion is a matter of following

Christ, being formed by his teaching and imitating his example. In time we become more Christlike and move towards that state of communion in which we can say, "I live, now not I, but Christ lives in me" (Gal. 2:20).

1. Affective Religion

Affective relationship to God in Christ Jesus is the totality of spiritual life. Love of God surpasses in importance all the worthy and more immediate goals preachers proclaim: religious observance, keeping the commandments, minimizing the suffering of others, attaining a high level of personal truth. The difficulty of proposing a love-based religion is that such a religion needs to draw life from within. How can anyone respond to a love (*redamare*) that has not been personally experienced? How can anyone be initiated into the mysteries of the spiritual world who steadfastly refuses to quit—be it ever so briefly—the world of tangible reality?[92]

Thomas Csordas has suggested that in a devotee's personal love for Jesus, there is also a love for one's deepest self, of which Jesus becomes either model or image.

> Jesus is the alterity of the self. . . . I am arguing that the capacity for intimacy begins with an existential coming to terms with the alterity of the self, and that the personal relation with Jesus is a metaphor for that condition of selfhood. This is the Jesus that speaks internally with the "still, small voice" within, and whose presence is an act of the imagination. . . . The vivid presence of Jesus in imaginal performance is a culturally specific way to complete this second foundational moment, providing an ideal Other to correspond to the self-presence that characterizes autobiographical memory.[93]

Csordas's etiology needs qualification (an *imagined* Jesus could equally be a vengeful and unlovable judge), and his conclusions apply only partially to spiritual experiences more advanced than those that are the object of his research. However, the idea that love for Jesus is co-extensive with love of my hidden self is worth retaining. It reinforces the traditional teaching that abandoning false selves and living from the heart is the most effective means of finding God. Or, more correctly, of allowing ourselves to be found by God. For a faithful Christian, self-knowledge leads almost inevitably to knowledge or experience of God. This linkage between love for the human Christ and self-acceptance is established by the impression that a lack of appropriate self-love prevents any real spiritual growth and is an almost certain indicator of an unfeeling and systemic rigorism.[94] Christianity is about loving God with a certain fullness of mind, heart, and spirit. It is about loving our neighbor as much as we love ourselves. First, we must love ourselves, and that usually means that we have already received from others the message that we are lovable.

2. Historical Development

It was in the age of the martyrs that the New Testament teaching on Christ-affectivity became crucial. Faced with persecution and the probability of torture and death, Christians of that era found that something more than mere ethical motivation was needed. Two things stand out in the contemporary accounts of martyrdom: the martyrs' effusive personal love for Christ combined with the desire to imitate him by sharing in his sufferings, and their spirit of profound joy that accepted pain and baffled unbelievers.

The spirituality propounded in narrative form in the *Acts* of the martyrs was the most lively expression available of evangelical life. Teachers such as Origen quickly applied it to conscientious followers of the gospel: "I have no doubt that these also are they who have taken up their cross and followed Christ."[95] Fervent Christian life, in general, and especially monastic life were viewed as "white martyrdom,"[96] and practical patience was understood as a participation in Christ's passion.

In the view of Claude Peifer, "monasticism grew out of the most devout circles of the second- and third-century Church, the virgins and ascetics, and was strongly marked with the imprint of the spirituality of martyrdom."[97] The workaday spirituality that powered fervent monastic lives was simply personal devotion to the person of Christ. If in the monasteries this *affectus cordis* was more ardent than in the Church in general, it was simply because an existence that was ordinary, obscure, and laborious needed greater interior stimulus if it were not to collapse into a sterile regime of pious inertia.

This love for Christ rose to a crescendo among the Cistercians of the twelfth century, who needed a strong counter-balance to the excess of fear prevailing in religious circles. The first generations of Cistercian monks were all adult recruits who were presumed, generally speaking, to have pursued lives of youthful self-indulgence with sufficient zest to warrant a radical conversion. In the monastery they lived a rugged macho existence with little comfort and a more-than-usual degree of bodily exertion and austerity. To service the interior needs of these tough young males a complementary spirituality developed, which has been described by Jean Leclercq as a "feminine" spirituality.

In the monasteries, personal love for Jesus was supplemented by a devotion to four feminine realities, made easier by the gender of the Latin words: *Anima, Sapientia, Ecclesia, Maria*. The monk's devotion to an interior life was governed by principles complementary to his masculine exterior life. The life of the soul was seen as running along a complementary track to the life of the body. It was understood as the search for Lady Wisdom or Sophia; devotion to Christ's bride, the Church; care of one's own soul and—beyond these hypostatizations—a deep personal attachment to Mary, not only as the mother of the historical Jesus, but also as a mother, advocate, and patron in one's own spiritual journey.

The Cistercian spirituality of this era was uncompromising in its demand for single-mindedness, expressed externally by a rigorous life that was the opposite of self-indulgence, and internally by an equally exigent pursuit of unblinking self-knowledge. Yet, at the level of personal experience, there is only tenderness, gentleness, and an overriding confidence in the all-accepting mercy of God: a soft spirituality but—be warned!—one that loses all meaning if separated from its hard tegument. Bernard often reminds us that in the house of Bethany there can be no Mary without Martha and Lazarus: The labor of penance and the generosity of service are the indispensable buttresses to the joy of contemplation.

The word that epitomizes this experience-oriented spirituality is *dulcedo*, sweetness. It is unfortunate that the term has become debased through the flowery excesses of pietism. Monastic life presupposes all sorts of external observances and deprivations, but these are secondary. What drives them is an untrammeled interior affectivity that has its focus on the person of Christ, but is necessarily both unconditional and unrestricted in those to whom it reaches out. This is not a grim life in which the monk labors at breaking his egotism as a convict might break rocks. It is more a matter of so allowing oneself to fall under the sway of the attractiveness of God that lesser realities lose their charm. At those moments when we let go of alternative satisfactions, God's presence activates the deepest zone of selfhood; something within us flares into life with an unpredictable intensity so that we experience ourselves as drawn to God, lost in God, one with God, divinized. We have tasted and seen for ourselves that the Lord is sweet.

3. The Qualities of Love for Christ

The spirituality of Christ's love both engages and satisfies affectivity. Embraced in its integrity it transforms a monk or nun into a great lover, less likely to succumb to the rigors of institutional sterility or to the more immediate enticements of sexual temptation. Here, however, we need to remind ourselves that a life built around desire for God and love for Jesus, is not an easy option. Any attempt to subvert its intrinsic challenge will produce unfortunate results—deep self-distortion and phoniness that open the door to all sorts of latent pathologies. When monastic tradition inculcates a personal love for Christ, this teaching needs to be seen in its integral context and not reduced to merely superficial devotionalism, even if it begins that way.

a) **Personal love for Jesus is fed by constant meditation on the Gospels.** It is necessary that it be based on more than our own psychological needs. We have to keep meeting Christ in all the changing circumstances of our life, reading the text of the Gospels closely in order to discover there new facets of the mystery that will help us to become more Christlike today. We will be surprised at how often we find ourselves attracted to aspects of the person and message of Jesus that we had not noticed hitherto, and this is a sign that we are making progress. If we are to have in us the mind and heart of Christ, ongoing raw contact with the text of the Gospels is necessary, detaching us from false pictures and building up in our memories an image of Christ that is authentic, energizing, and suitable for our level of spiritual understanding.

b) **Personal love for Jesus goes hand in hand with the actualization of our deeper self.** We all have the experience of friendship. What is so fulfilling about having good

friends is not only that it is pleasing to be in the company
of such wonderful people, but also the fact that their
interaction awakens in us something that had been
otherwise unrealized or dormant. In their presence we
are more alive. When they are absent we go back to
being "ourselves" again. If they die something in us
dies also. One of the great insights of the spiritual life
is the recognition that there is in us a double level of
selfhood—one fashioned by the common events of our
external history, the other hidden, the fruit of inner
experience. What is described as "spiritual progress"
is usually a matter of being somewhat free from the
necessities imposed by the "outer self" and free for the
flowering of the "inner self."[98] The impact that Jesus had
on his immediate circle of acquaintance was to awaken
in them a consciousness of their own spiritual potential:
Fishermen were no longer constrained within the limits
of their craft or social standing; they became disciples,
apostles, missionaries, preachers, miracle-workers, and
martyrs. Others of their ilk remained fishermen all their
lives. What made the difference was that Jesus roused in
the Twelve a boldness to be something more than they
had been in the past. The deep self had been woken
up and was ready for action. The same happens to us,
though the contact is less immediate. When Jesus begins
to emerge from the pages of the Gospel as a real person
who engages us, then something begins to stir in our
hearts that leads us in directions previously unconsidered.
In the presence of Jesus the deeper, inner self comes to the
surface and has a chance to refashion our lives.

c) **Personal love for Jesus demands an equal measure of
self-disregard.** John the Baptist proclaimed: "He must
increase; I must decrease" (Jn. 3:30). So, as the inner
self becomes more powerful, the outer self loses its
total control over our lives. "The external self is fading

away but our inner [self] is being renewed day by day"
(2 Cor. 4:16). No one can exist in an affective void; the
only force that can bring calm to the chaos of conflicting
loves is a love that outclasses them all. It is a matter of
fighting fire with the fieriest fire of all. When the love of
Jesus draws forth the best in us the lower appetites go
into recession. It is not that we conquer them; they simply
lose their capacity to charm us. We lose interest in what
hitherto enchanted us. Of course the conversion is never
absolute; there is always plenty of scope for backsliding.
But there is a discernible direction in life that leads away
from self-centeredness. A devotional life that coexists
with an unchallenged concern for personal comfort and
advancement is likely to be spurious. The measures of
love's authenticity are stern. They include the following:

- detachment from material resources and
  advantages,
- capacity to endure or embrace pain happily—
  patience (7:35–42),
- ruthless self-honesty and a progressive openness
  to direction (7:44–48),
- determination to hide its virtue from public sight
  (4:62),
- generosity in serving others, and
- conscious union with the Church.

Such a heart is predisposed to experience the full intensity
of love for Jesus. In most cases the behavioral patterns
listed above are not the conditions or causes of that love,
but its effects. "Love is poured forth in our hearts by the
Holy Spirit who is given to us" (Rom. 5:5); in those open
to its influence such infused charity begins to reshape
their lives.

d) **Personal love for Jesus, if it is genuine, opens the frontiers of the heart to other persons.** Love is, of its nature, indivisible. Either we love whatever good we experience or we are indifferent to it. When authentic love enters our lives everyone is the beneficiary of it. Far from being an exclusive focusing on a single person, love, as distinct from infatuation, makes us appreciative of the qualities of all around us. That is why, in the musicals of the 1950s, when people fell in love, they went singing and dancing down the street, astonishing everyone with their unaccustomed benevolence. We cannot love Jesus unless we also are drawn to love his other friends. This means more than vague goodwill to a faceless multitude. It means recognizing the Christ in all whom we encounter in our daily lives. It is not a matter of forcing ourselves to be positive out of love for Jesus, but if our love is genuine we cannot help being struck by the goodness and lovableness of all around us. Beginners in the spiritual life often withdraw from others whose spirituality does not, they believe, match their own. Those in the higher reaches tend, as Benedict notes, to be highly conscious of their own defects (7:62–66) and be lost in admiration at the holiness of others. The implications of Matthew 25 are clear: We must see Christ even in the least worthy. Love of Christ confirms us in our appreciation of others and in our affective outreach toward them. It is no longer "us" and "them." When we love, the defenses go down and the heart is more open to be captivated by those around us.

e) **Personal love for Jesus, if it is genuine, is able to withstand the vicissitudes inherent in every interpersonal relationship.** Because the relationship with Jesus is dynamic, it involves us in the uncertainty that springs from not being in total control. Spiritual growth works through change, but we instinctively resist change when it involves sacrificing the known for the unknown. So we must endure storms—some of which may drive us to rebellion. There are mysterious passages in life in which we move away from that which is pleasantly familiar and are inescapably confronted with the dread of a future that escapes our control. For Bernard, this alternation of experience was the criterion by which the reality of spiritual life could be assessed. The sign of God's active presence in the soul is an unpredictable mélange of positive and negative experience.[99] Every human life is marked by times of suffering in which only endurance is possible. The surest indication of responsiveness to grace is an uncomplaining serenity in the face of such disempowering reversals. Real love is prepared to batten down the hatches and weather the storms, not regarding the present pain as typical, but reframing it within the context of a lifetime's experience.[100] Appreciation of the eschatological character of Christian life leads to a more mellow assessment of the importance of present difficulties. In the course of a lifelong dedication to the love of Christ, there will be many qualitatively different demands and experiences, the meaning of which will be apparent only in retrospect. The feeling of love flourishes when the object of love is present. When the loved one is absent, we experience not only the positive yearning of desire, but also its negative sense of emptiness and meaninglessness. Both presence and absence have something to contribute to our story; both are occasions for the exercise of love.

f) **Personal love for Jesus, if it is genuine, has the capacity to rebound after major betrayal.** We do not go to God in a single leap. Notwithstanding the affective intensity that often surrounds the experience of conversion, it is easy enough to slide back into an empty indifference in which we are assailed with a new vigor by temptations that we thought we had outgrown. In fact the strength of the experience convinced us that we could not be moved. This false sense of security is "the mother of negligence and the generator of carelessness."[101] And so we are expelled from the easeful garden of delight and recommitted to spiritual warfare. This normalization does not feel like an improvement, but it is. One of the most puzzling things in spiritual progress is that a point is reached when all that has been achieved must be abandoned. At a certain point, love for God can go no further, until it discovers the unconditional nature of the divine regard—and that means letting go of any notion of personal entitlement to love. We fail in what matters most to us, and we are close to losing our nerve and giving up the struggle. A mid-journey collapse is not uncommon.[102] In fact, for Bernard, it is unavoidable: *necesse est.*[103] Strangely enough, if we survive the period of our infidelity our response to God's love is both stronger and deeper—and much more realistic.

g) **Personal love for Jesus, if it is genuine, matures with the person—emotionally and intellectually.** Sentiment has a large role to play in the initial stages of love's evolution. This principle was clearly enunciated by Bernard in his treatise *On the Lovableness of God.*[104] This preliminary stage of sentimental devotion is a necessary point of departure for all spiritual development. It serves as a point of departure and, like all beginnings, it needs eventually to be left behind. One who does not rise to the challenges of self-forgetful love can easily be diverted into the byways of sentimentalism and kitsch. Phony pietism is not personal devotion to Christ, but a saccharine substitute that compensates for the absence of the real thing. Split off from the reality of everyday behavior, its lack of substance is frequently demonstrated by its easy cohabitation with the hard-nosed authoritarianism not uncommon among career churchmen. On the other hand, it is fatal to espouse a feelingless religion, so purified of sentiment that it becomes sterile. Post-Cartesian dualism, pietism (in its various forms), and the spurious commercialized piety of nineteenth-century prayer books have made us suspicious of any practice or formula that touches the feelings, but have offered us no alternatives. This has led to a "piety void" in which many, by losing faith in particular practices, have eventually lost interest in pursuing a spiritual life.

h) **Personal love for Jesus is wholesome.** First, it is not a respectable avenue for radical self-rejection. In such an unhealthy situation, Christ is loved, not because he is "like us in all things" but because he is utterly different. The ideals projected onto Christ, and governing our iconography, can be a subterfuge for a non-acceptance of our own humanity. We punish ourselves for being what we are by conjuring up a "perfect human being" who is more like an angel than a man. The heresy of Docetism is never far away from us. In striving to conform ourselves to this impossible ideal of super-humanity, we sink further into desperation and compound our self-rejection.[105] So painful is this situation that such devotion is marginalized and has no impact on how we live. Second, and less common, it can happen that love of Jesus may need to be protected from sexual pathologies. The focus in contemplation is not the imagined body of the man Jesus, but the ascended and glorified Christ, spiritually present at all points of space and time, but especially present in the deepest caverns of the human spirit. It is the forever-incarnate Word who is the "bridegroom" of the soul—*anima* being considered female. Mystical writers use the language not only of courtship, but also of sexual intercourse to describe the union realized in the contemplative act, although translators often water this down to prevent offense to pious ears. The point about such language is that it is metaphorical, because what is being described is meta-experiential.

Why so many cautionary remarks? The following of Jesus that love for him inspires is never without hardship. The Gospels leave us in no doubt about this. Therefore, those of us who are a bit slack may look for an easier way that provides us with comfort without challenge. A sentimental, feel-good devotion, full of verbal effusions but not impacting on our blind spots or hidden vices is not merely useless, it is positively harmful. It insulates us against the need for ongoing conversion and so convinces us of our own rightness that we become very hard on others. And all the while we think we are on the right track. Genuine love for Jesus is an austere, battle-ready reality that constantly summons us to self-transcendence and postpones until eternity the full enjoyment of what God's love promises us.

11 | *Contemplation*

With hearts expanded by love's
sweetness which is beyond words
RB PROL. 49

Most of us need to be careful that the Christocentric
character of our spiritual life, so evident in its
early phases, is not lost through inattention on our
part. Friendship with Christ needs to be maintained and
strengthened through time given to prayer. Without regular
prayer interpersonal kindness and service decline into routine
civility, intentionality becomes diffuse, and moral behavior
loses its vertical component. Goodness becomes a matter of
mere ethics and, thus, is not sustainable for long. We are
Christians, and the badge we wear is Christlike behavior.
Such a way of life, however, loses its hold over us if it ceases
to be Christ-centered and becomes mere role-playing or
philanthropy. Prayer, by which we maintain contact with
the invisible realities of spiritual life, is essential.

The dogged grind of regular prayer sets the stage for
occasional moments in which we experience intimate
communion with God. It is not that there are techniques
that guarantee that this will happen whenever we feel
like it. The dynamics of prayer are different. Seemingly
earthbound prayer has the capacity to grind away at our

delusions until we are free of them, so that sometimes, to use John Cassian's image, we lift off, like a feather caught by a sudden gust of wind. These moments of meta-experience make worthwhile all the labor of virtue and the struggle against temptations. They are signposts that point us toward the goal and assure us that, despite our sense of being lost, we are still moving in the right direction.

1. Mystical Monks?

The Jesuit theologian Karl Rahner suggested that the Christian of the future must be a mystic.[106] Perhaps the time has come to emphasize more blatantly the mystical and contemplative dimension of Benedictine life, to cherish the theory and practice of our tradition and to communicate it more boldly to those who come to us for formation. It is certainly an integral part of our charism but, at times, it tends to be overlarded by less important emphases. Without an explicit contemplative orientation, monastic asceticism makes little sense, and the demands of low-impact living seem unreasonable. Robbed of their finality, monastic observances are either watered down or become the source of anger, sadness, and escapist behavior on the part of disgruntled monks and nuns who claim not to understand why they cannot be allowed to live "normal" lives.

It is a pity that in common ecclesiastical parlance "contemplative" is used in a quasi-juridical sense, to describe groups with no external apostolate. Communities of the Benedictine tradition have often been slow to appropriate the term "contemplative" because they do not recognize themselves adequately described in such Vatican texts as *Sponsa Christi* and *Venite Seorsum*, particularly in the matter of enclosure. In addition, some of the early writings of Thomas Merton and others have tended to make "contemplation" seem like an alien and elitist notion that pays too little honor to the monastic insistence that prayer is embedded in the commonplace realities of community work, worship, and interaction. Yes, many communities that follow Benedict's Rule have a sound tradition of dedication to works of various kinds, but the best of them also insist on the priority of prayer.

Consciously accepting the contemplative finality of monastic life is undoubtedly good for morale, but it also assists in public relations. Those considering monastic life today seem less interested in fuzzy goals and multiple options—they have grown up in such conditions and have experienced for themselves how limited is their value. It seems to me that many inquirers are seeking clear and attractive priorities, appropriate communal structures that express these values, plus an abundance of good example. It is like the old lady who remarked after hearing the bishop read an eloquent sermon verbatim, "If he can't remember it himself, how can he expect us to?" If we do not know where we are going, how can we help others to go to the same destination?

We have to be aware that some of the language of our tradition has been debased in recent centuries. The traditional insistence on humility and obedience seems oppressive to many modern readers until they receive some assistance in interpreting the Rule. And we are all aware that giving too much centrality to institutional obedience has often led to an abuse of power that brings nobody closer to God. In visiting a Buddhist monastery some time ago, it struck me powerfully that today the ideal of self-realization is a much more attractive foundation on which to build the image of monastic life than the narrower way of obedience to a superior, seen as a means of being conformed to the will of God. Self-realization is patently a way of growth; obedience seems only a way of diminishment that takes considerable spiritual maturity to appreciate. Needless to say, both aspects of monastic life are essential. Nobody can escape the mystery of the Cross. We can, however, follow the example of Jesus in the Gospel and reveal this aspect of discipleship further down the track. Without weakening Benedict's injunction that novices be forewarned of hard times ahead, we may get better results from a more heuristic approach to diminishment in general and obedience in particular. Meanwhile we insist that monastic life is a road that leads to union with God. Over the years those who follow this path will enter more experientially into the Mystery communicated in Baptism—they will become mystics.

The word "mysticism" rings alarm bells. For many it conjures up images of parapsychological or pathological phenomena. Most monastic guest houses are occasionally burdened with self-styled mystics; some are harmless, some are mad, others are dangerous because they attempt to make disciples of the gullible. A few become nuisances because they do not respect appropriate boundaries and start interfering in the community itself. All this is a pity because such aberrations give mysticism a bad name, and monastic life does not make a great deal of sense unless mystical contemplation is seen as its goal. It is not a matter of cause and effect: if you do certain things then you will experience mystical union with God. The contrary is true. We already have found what we seek, but do not know it. Through baptism we have been invited into communion with God at the level of being. The life of grace is nothing more than living out that filial relationship with God. Mostly, however, this dynamism operates at a non-conscious level. What monastic life offers is a slow process of purifying the heart so that it can perceive the deep mystery in which we have been immersed. The negative aspects of monastic observance and spiritual growth are the pangs that accompany this necessary transformation. Returning to the "three renunciations" of Paphnutius, we recall that the motivation to give up family and possessions and engage in the ascetical life is the assurance that, with God's grace, this is the way by which we enter into full awareness of the mystery of God. Such meta experience is less unusual   than we might expect, even though many lack the vocabulary to describe what has transpired.[107]

Benedict himself takes for granted that such a transformation of consciousness is the normal result of a life lived in conformity with God through faith, obedience, patience, and perseverance. When we amputate the ultimate goal of monastic observances we have nothing left to inspire optimism and buoyancy. It is simply a *via negativa* without even the breathing spaces (*respiria*) that Western tradition has led us to expect during the hard slog of the journey toward God.

2. Prayer Integrated in Living

For those unenthusiastic about the term "mystical," it is important to understand its origins. It is related to the word "mystery," a term that means more than a puzzle to be solved. A mystery, in the strict sense of the word, is a reality that is eminently reasonable, but cannot be circumscribed by reason. A famous (and probably apocryphal) story is told of Augustine walking by the seashore trying to get his powerful intellect to unlock the meaning of the Trinity. Seeing a small boy trying, by means of his little bucket, to empty the ocean into a hole he had dug, Augustine laughed—only to be told that this was a more realistic project than his attempt to master the mystery of God. When we speak of mysticism or meta-experience we are speaking of our capacity to be drawn sometimes into a zone beyond the familiar world of space and time, a zone in which all our interior faculties come alive. What transpires during those graced moments is beyond language. God is a reality that we can never explain or prove. This is what we mean by "mystery." The Incarnation is a mystery, and so is the Atonement. So is the Church. So are the sacraments and the sacred liturgy. None of these realities lack reasonableness, but not one of them can ever be fully captured by reason. The most that can be done is to give a dim sketch by means of symbol and metaphor.

Our experience of prayer is our entry into the realm of mystery. If you like, it is stepping out of space and time into eternity, where we are conscious only that our spirits are being fed. It is this heavenly nourishment that energizes our efforts to live according to the impossible precepts of the gospel. It is not only when times are hard that we are sustained by prayer: Only to those who pray is it possible to keep stretching out beyond ordinary comfort zones to a closer following of Jesus. Monastic life is not possible without prolonged dedication to prayer; where prayer is lacking, commitment falters and life begins to fall apart.

However, contemplative practice is not without its ambiguities. It is made up of a large portion of what Dom Hubert Van Zeller termed "the prayer of stupidity," when one does not know for sure if any prayer is taking place, since all seems to be flatness, distraction, and a restlessness that makes continuance difficult. This is a normal sense of anomie, since one is entering a foreign country where, as John of the Cross pointed out, the old rules do not apply. We are strangers in paradise, and we feel somewhat lost. In at least one Middle English author the word "mystical" seems to have been connected with the idea of mist and hence cloud. We cannot see clearly the way ahead, and we sense that control is being wrested from our grasp. What is experienced in contemplation can never be seen directly or clearly stated in words, because conceptualization and language are inadequate, just as a comic book version of the theory of relativity would be. No doubt that is why Benedict uses the term "ineffable": to indicate that the taste of divine sweetness defies human description.

It follows from this that there can be no permanent structures or techniques that will infallibly lead to a sense of closeness to God. This is simply because there is no standard or universal "mystical" experience. We are speaking of a relationship, and our relationship with God is determined by where we are at a particular time. When we are in a different space, our prayer is different. John Cassian, Benedict's own master of prayer, is very clear about this.

> I believe that it is impossible to grasp all the different forms of prayer without great purity of heart and soul. There are as many forms of prayer as there are states of soul or, rather, there are as many as the totality of states experienced by all souls together. We are not able to experience all the various kinds of prayer due to our inner debility, nevertheless, let us try to go through those which we know from our own far-from-extraordinary experience.
>
> Prayer is fashioned anew from moment to moment according to the measure in which the mind is purified and according to the situation in which it finds itself, whether this be the result of external contingencies or of its own doing. It is certain, moreover, that nobody is ever able to keep praying in the same way. A person prays in a certain manner when cheerful and in another when weighed down by sadness or a sense of hopelessness. When one is flourishing spiritually, prayer is different from when one is oppressed by the extent of one's struggles. One prays in this manner when seeking pardon for sins, and in that manner when asking for some grace or virtue or the elimination of a particular vice. Sometimes prayer is conditioned by compunction,

occasioned by the thought of hell and the fear of judgment; at other times it is aflame with hope and desire for the good things to come. People pray in one manner when they are in dangerous straits and in another when enjoying quiet and security. Prayer is sometimes illumined by the revelation of heavenly mysteries but, at other times, one is forced to be content with the sterile practice of virtue and the experience of aridity.[108]

What this boils down to is that while we can be emphatic about the contemplative finality of monastic life, we cannot promise that the goal will be infallibly reached if a person perseveres in particular practices. Some people are exasperated by this typically Benedictine reluctance to be prescriptive when it comes to practice of prayer. This is not a matter of ignorance of various techniques or confusion about means and ends. This slowness to impose particular practices is the result of a realistic sensitivity to the differences among persons, the subtle changes that accompany spiritual growth, and the sovereign freedom of God to make light of any human construct.

Early in the last century Abbot Cuthbert Butler published a book with the title *Western Mysticism* relaying the mystical teaching of Augustine, Gregory the Great, and Bernard of Clairvaux. What is common to the approach taken by these authors, and to Western Fathers generally, is the insistence that prayer comes as part of a package. It is embedded in a network of supportive practices: interior and exterior, individual and communal, spontaneous and routine. Most likely if prayer is not functioning well it is because of some discordance or imbalance between the different elements of Christian living: too much of this and too little of that. The remedy is found less in fine-tuning prayer itself, as in ensuring that all the other "implements of the spiritual craft" are in good condition and are being used as appropriate. In fact, we will find that experiences of dysphoria during prayer are often due to interpersonal difficulties, lack of self-care, or defective obedience. The seeming failure of prayer is not a penalty or punishment, but merely a signal that something needs attention. Even though it is comfortless our prayer is successful, if it brings us more fully into the realm of truth. Just as aches and pains alert us to muscular over-exertion, so, when in prayer we experience ourselves at a great distance from God, we are being invited to re-assess our priorities in living and probably to modify some aspects of our daily conduct.

I was very impressed, many years ago, reading the views of a world-famous nutritionist. He was of the opinion that most people, in order to be healthy, need do no more than eat a varied diet. An unhealthy diet for him was one in which, by necessity or choice, the range of foods was limited. Given a wide variety of different foodstuffs, the body can forage for what it needs without being oppressed by too much of anything. He was dubious about the value of strict diets or dietary supplements because, when it comes to trace elements, we do not know enough about what the body really needs to be able to provide it.

Our prayer draws what it needs from the variety of our daily experiences. This is why I have reservations about the wisdom of concentrating the bulk of one's spiritual effort in a particular practice, such as the rigorous repetition of a mantra such as *Marana tha* or the Jesus Prayer, valuable though these may be for some people some of the time. The experience of many monks and nuns is that their awareness of the closeness of God occurs as often outside formal prayer as inside it: at work, in caring for others, in admiring the scenery, even in sleep. God will not be organized. If our expectations of prayer are built on the hypothesis of God's predictability, our only certainty is that we will be disappointed.

3. The Variety of Mystical Experience

Because our moments of more intense awareness of God's presence seem spontaneously to leap out of the ordinariness of daily living, they are beyond our direct causation. As a result we often are slow to own these flickers of divine intimacy, because we did nothing to bring them about. Yet though they happen infrequently and are gone before we can scrutinize them, these "stirrings" (as the Author of *The Cloud of Unknowing* termed them) are very important. They encourage us and confirm to us that a particular action or attitude is potentially transparent, leached of self-importance, so that through it the glory of the Lord may shine. What bothers us is the humility of such experiences. There is no "objective" content, nothing to recount afterwards, just a modified awareness independent from sense experience or logical deduction, yet strangely warm and personal. We cannot capture these moments of grace or preserve them in amber; we cannot gather them in with our rational mind and submit them to analysis. Like sparks in stubble they rise from nowhere and vanish.

When the divine light shines upon us it is refracted by the prism of our own personal history. This means that if we try to paint a picture of what we have experienced, the result may seem no more than a reflection of our own interior images. Variation may be due to differences in the way our minds operate. Many people translate the experience into something visual, but for others it is a voice they hear or a concept that presents itself. One may expect different degrees of emotional intensity. There may be a variety of psychological determinants. One who was mother-deprived may experience these moments of spiritual awakening as a maternal presence, as may another person who had a strong exposure to maternal love in infancy. The same can be said about paternal images of God. There may even be deep, personal reasons why some choose to describe what they have felt in abstract and metaphysical language. Others may use language based on Scripture, or belonging to a school of theology or devotion. What one person interprets as the work of the Holy Spirit, another may ascribe to the intervention of angels or the intercession of the saints. The experience is one thing, the faltering attempts to explain it are something else. Those involved in inter-religious dialogue often report great harmony among participants, so long as they remain at the level of experience; as soon as theology enters the conversation, divisions multiply.

What I am suggesting is that we need to be cautious in assigning absolute significance to our interpretations of religious experience. It is true that sometimes these spiritual events can serve to mirror some subliminal reality within our own spirits; what we see or hear needs, however, to be submitted to discernment—by ourselves and by others. Where there is question of simple consolation, there is no harm in accepting it with gratitude. But if what we have experienced seems to impel us towards a particular course of action, especially if it involves a radical change of direction, then we need to seek counsel. If we become convinced that we have a message for somebody else, I think we need to be very circumspect. I may be a bit prejudiced, but I tend to think that any reading of our experience that sends us off on some prophetic crusade is unlikely to come from God and more probably comes from a deranged mind.

The fact of the matter is that, at a secondary level, religious experience is not immune from silliness. A genuine experience can sometimes interact with our own neuroses to cause a considerable wastage of time and diversion of energy; it may even have results that are harmful to us or to others. Such is the fragility of our human condition. It is because of such aberrations that many stolid Christians are suspicious of anything to do with "mysticism" and try to maintain an even level of neutrality in their own religious sentiments. Beware of this also. Some people feel obliged to restrict themselves to "rational" religion so that the chances of being led astray by emotion are reduced. More often than not the result is chronic aridity. Trying to exclude feeling from religion is as silly as allowing oneself to be dominated by it. As in everything else, common sense, balance, and good advice will serve us best.

A mystical experience is one in which there is no direct causation within the spatio-temporal universe. It is the fleeting imprint of eternity on our dull awareness. It cannot be known directly. Its genuineness is attested by its effects. Meta-experience does not fall within the ambit of personal control, and so there is an overwhelming quality about it that makes those who experience it diffident to flaunt it. In simpler terms, far from making them proud, it tends to induce a deep sense of humility. There is a great deal of energy contained within a brief moment, so that often a person is empowered to do something long resisted as too difficult.

The intensity of such experience cannot be measured by the degree of drama accompanying it. As we all know, some people experience life as grand opera, with soaring highs and terrifying lows. The ordinary rarely intrudes on their passionate existence. A day without a crisis is unbearable. For such people, religious experience also is dramatic. For those who are solidly phlegmatic, however, even strong moments of divine intimacy rarely cause a ripple on the surface of their equanimity. For the rest of us, who are in-between, God comes into our lives with a middle-level impact. It is as though the divine visitations are accommodated to suit our own particular disposition. For all, the two criteria of authenticity mentioned above are equally valid: humility and energy for good.

What are some concrete examples of everyday mystical experience? Let me list some and say a little about each.

a) **Conversion:** As we have spoken about above, whether it be cumulative or sudden, this experience opens our eyes, allowing us to evaluate issues differently, and gives us the energy to change the direction of our life.

b) **Vocation:** This experience gives us the courage to embark on a new life that has God at its center, helping us to accept the inevitable sacrifices involved, and allowing us to yield control of our life to God and to others.

c) **Compunction:** In the ancient tradition this is more than our feeling-response to the realization of our sinfulness. It is whatever "through God's grace, is able to arouse the soul from its sleepiness and half-heartedness."[109]

d) **Searching:** There are many people today who are "looking for something" that their own culture does not give them. These pilgrims of the Absolute have been touched by some intangible Reality, and they are restless until they can establish a more permanent relationship.

e) **Patience:** This is reckoned by Benedict as the key to everything (Prol. 50). We often observe this quality in faith-filled people—how steadfast they are in times of change, how courageous when affliction strikes, how hopeful when everything is hopeless. It is obvious that such endurance comes from an inner strength that is much more powerful than mere character.

f) **Self-Transcendence:** Those who live forgetful of the demands of the superficial self and responsive to the deeper calling of spiritual reality show by their behavior that they have tasted for themselves the goodness of the Lord; henceforth nothing else has the power to satisfy them for long.

g) **Love:** Sometimes we can be possessed by a love that seems unconditional, that has no boundaries, and is able to embrace even those who act against us. It is unlike our love for those nearest and dearest in that it is proactive, making lovable those whom otherwise we would have considered unlovable, turning enemies into friends, and embracing the whole world with the arms of our concern.

h) **Communion:** Many of us experience long periods in which prayer seems fairly unproductive. Yet, even in our gloomiest moods, we have to admit that there have been breathing spaces. God seems to have visited us. We felt our own will becoming conformed to God's. We felt drawn out of ourselves in desire and longing, and in a sense that God was our true home. Despite the prevailing distance, we experienced at least moments of communion with God. "I have seen God face to face and my soul is alive," as the Latin translation literally renders Genesis 32:30.

Such experiences are common enough among those who have chosen to assign importance to living a spiritual life, and to those who have embraced a religious or monastic vocation. I consider them to be "mystical experiences," even though they are not accompanied with the fireworks commonly associated with that term. This is not to say they are defective or inferior to visions, revelations, and prophecies. They are more profound and long-lasting, and they are the ordinary means by which the mystery of Christ-life is continued in our world.

12 | *Holiness*

*Do not wish to be called holy before
you are; first be holy that you may
more truly be said to be so.*
RB 4:62

In the Middle Ages, a monastery was often described simply as an ecclesia, a church. The use of such a term underlined the fact that what was in question was a holy community—that those who lived there were, in the usage of the New Testament, "saints"—men and women dedicated to living holy lives. Listen to Bernard reminding his monks of this.

> This community is made up not of the wicked but of saints, religious men, those who are full of grace and worthy of blessing. You come together to hear the word of God, you gather to sing praise, to pray, to offer adoration. This is a consecrated assembly, pleasing to God and familiar with the angels. Therefore, brothers, stand fast in reverence, stand with care and devotion of mind, especially in the place of prayer and in this school of Christ where the Spirit is heard.[110]

When prayer ceased to be a priority, when monastic observance became slack, and monasteries grew rich and powerful, holiness ceased to be a visible attribute of such communities. They degenerated and became corporations or institutions of one sort of another. As a result their role and function in the Church and in society became less obvious, and monks and nuns themselves became vague about the ultimate finality of their vocation.

1. *Communio* and *Communitas*

One of the great temptations for any community that is relatively clear about its ideals is that its cardinal values may be systematized in a way that pays scant regard to persons. The values are fine, and the structures designed to express and communicate the values are objectively good. The problem is that they may not necessarily be serving their purpose within this particular group of people. Sometimes a charismatic figure or founder can hold the group together by force of character, but, often enough, when the leadership passes to a successor, rumblings begin to be heard. It may be only one or two people who marginalize themselves, but they are expressing a wider and deeper dissatisfaction.

Comparing the Rule of Augustine to that of Benedict we notice in the former a much stronger emphasis on the theme of "one heart and one mind." It is true that in the finale to Benedict's Rule we find something of a re-reading of the earlier chapters in more personal terms, but there is plenty in the Rule that, for the literal-minded, could provide a justification for setting up a "total institution." Indeed some of the autocratic religious superiors of the nineteenth and twentieth centuries saw no harm in taking that particular route, somewhat unaware of the harm they were doing and the pain they were inflicting. The chaos that followed the termination of their authoritarian regimes is sufficient proof that the values so long trumpeted had scarcely taken root.

By the twelfth century there was a greater appreciation of the role of subjective experience in monasteries. The early Cistercians, in particular, tried to make of their communities schools of love, where it was recognized that full human and spiritual development was coterminous with the practical will to love and be loved. Such fraternal affection was not mere sentiment. It was contextualized by a common purpose and the acceptance of common means to attain the monastic goal of union with God. It was the sort of love that develops among like-minded travelers on the same journey.

> [Christ] does not like corners; private places do not please him. He stands in the midst: discipline, the common life and common pursuits: these are the things that bring him pleasure.[111]

Aelred's teaching on spiritual and monastic friendship is based on similar presuppositions. The discovery of a compatible person serious about the same priorities can be the foundation of a close relationship that owes more to the spirit than to the flesh. This is a love that comes from the will; it is powered on our side by an active faith and on God's by the inpouring of the Holy Spirit.

For the most part we do not choose those among whom we live. We belong to a community of faith that draws together persons of different personalities and dispositions. We are of different generations and levels of culture. Ordinary affinity is not enough to sustain us in mutual fidelity for a lifetime, and close living is a sure guarantee that even the slightest foible or failing will not go unnoticed or unremarked. The love that covers such a multitude of imperfections needs to borrow heavily from God's unconditional love for us; it is only thus that it can be simultaneously sincere, heartfelt, and all-forgiving.

This commingling of characters is not typical only of pluralist modernity. St. Aelred speaks humorously of the different characters that formed the community at Rievaulx, taking as his starting point the text of Isa. 11:6, about the wolf lying down with the lamb:

> Consider how God has gathered you together in this place, from vastly different regions and from different lifestyles. One of you, when he was in the world, was like a lion, who despised others and thought himself better than them because of his pride and riches. Another was like a wolf, who lived from robbery, whose only interest was how to steal the property of others. A leopard is an animal marked by variety: such were some of you [who lived] by your wits, through deception and fraud. Furthermore there were many in this community who were foul because of their sexual sins. Such as these were like goats—because goats are foul animals. There were some of you who lived innocent lives when you were in the world; they may well be compared to lambs. There were others who were like sheep because you lived a simple life. Look now, brothers, and see with how much concord and peace God has gathered all these into one common life. Here the wolf lives with the lamb; he eats and drinks with the lamb and does him no harm, but loves him greatly.[112]

Unity does not derive from a common background; it comes from an act of will by which each renounces individualism and strives to live in concord. Community of will has a double function: It serves as a check to self-will and it creates a climate of harmony that makes the cohabitation of brothers a good and pleasant thing. It creates an affective community where differences are neither denied nor suppressed. Any tendency to fragmentation is subverted by the "glue of love."

> Meanwhile the Spirit of wisdom is not only single but also manifold, compacting interior realities into unity, but in judgment making distinction among exterior things. Both are recommended to you in the primitive Church where "the multitude of believers had one heart and one soul" and "distribution was made to everyone according as each had need." So there should be a unity of souls among us, my friends. Hearts should be united by loving the one thing, seeking the one thing, adhering to the one thing and, among ourselves, being of the same mind. Thus external division will involve no danger and produce no scandal. Each will have his own field of tolerance and sometimes his own opinion about what is to be done in earthly matters. Furthermore, there will even be different gifts of grace and not all members will appear to follow the same course of action. Nevertheless interior unity and unanimity will gather and bind together this multiplicity with the glue of love and the bond of peace.[113]

As Baldwin of Forde implied in the treatise already quoted, *communio* is the heart of the Church and of every monastic community. This being so, relationships are an important part of the cenobitic dynamic. Sometimes you hear opinions implying that the only way to preserve unity is to avoid relationship: Members of the community are encouraged to build their personal space and to go their own way; serious conversation and community dialogues are avoided since they are regarded as a potential threat to peace and harmony, although it is unclear what sort of unity is thus threatened. Unity cannot be built by avoidance. Differences need to be positively reconciled. For this to happen there must exist relationships of sufficient depth to mine the deep zones where unity already exists. This is not achieved easily, but there is no other way. We are a community because we have made an act of the will to become a community, with God's grace. Such an outcome is more than mere serendipity. It comes about by faith. The community it creates is essentially a holy community.

If it is true that a community is bound together by a spider's web of interlocking relationships among its members, then it must be obvious that any defect or disruption in these linkages will endanger the community's well-being. This, no doubt, is why many of our most persistent temptations occur in the area of community relationships. And the area where dissension is most keenly felt in many communities is, undoubtedly, the liturgy.

2. The Primacy of Liturgy

It happened that the global trend towards secularization, expressed most dramatically in the "Death of God" movement, coincided with the period of post-Conciliar renewal of religious life.[114] It is, perhaps, to be regretted that elements of what was termed "secularization theology" unthinkingly came to be incorporated in the process of reformation and renewal. The total effect of this was the loss from religious life of many purely "sacred" observances, on the grounds that they lacked relevance to the contemporary world. Forty years later, we may need to embark on a process to recover a sense of the sacred—in effect, to desecularize or resacralize monastic life. It may be that in this realm also "God often reveals what is best to the young" (3:3).[115]

Monastic communities generally resisted secularizing trends better than most, partly due to the central position occupied by the Work of God and the relatively important place assigned to minor community rituals. Resisting a trend, especially when it means retaining elements with a whiff of the archaic about them, is hard work, and we may perhaps have experienced wave after wave of the same complaints that we are not more "normal." Inevitably some erosion occurs. Even the liturgy can be contaminated by foreign intrusions representing beliefs and values that are discordant with its true nature and with the character of a Benedictine community, and not consonant with our long tradition of communal worship.[116]

The celebration of the Liturgy of the Hours with the customary degree of solemnity demands nowadays a fair amount of energy, especially since the structure and texts of the liturgy are no longer a universal given and not every culture evinces the same facility for ritual. Although circumstances vary, there is a certain expectation that monasteries following the Benedictine Rule will have a liturgy in which maximum participation is combined with some degree of professionalism. For such a celebration to go beyond mere performance so that it also belongs to the local community and expresses its inner character, the community needs to have attained a "critical mass" that entails the following:

a) a certain size of community,
b) the necessary range of liturgical skills,
c) a generous portion of time available both for preparation and for celebration,
d) a good capacity for dialogue and consensus that leads to a liturgy acceptable to all and facilitates a certain unity of heart, and
e) the fundamental beliefs and values to sustain a corporate commitment to the communal celebration of the Liturgy of the Hours.

Such resources were once nearly universal. Now monastic demographics have changed and communities operate on a more human scale, sometimes because of choice and sometimes simply because of reduced recruitment. This means that grand liturgy is simply not always possible or desirable. A different style of liturgical celebration will necessarily be envisaged. It seems likely that changes in the liturgy will either reflect or foreshadow changes in the nature and dynamics of community life. The important thing is that whatever its shape, the community liturgy continues to play an important role, even at the cost of some sacrifice. In extreme situations there may be the risk that in the process of adaptation, the Work of God loses its effective priority. Liturgy could become a side show that absorbs little of the community's time or resources and may eventually be regarded as more or less optional.

Benedict's insistence on the priority of the Work of God (43:3) is not negotiable. The Liturgy of the Hours serves as an important structural element in the monastic day, no matter what size the community is or what its situation. It is a concrete means of re-injecting prayer into the daily round, calling the monk or nun to be mindful of the ultimate meaning of and direction of their life and providing a pause that refreshes. Precious time and energy given to the Divine Office is a clear signal about the finality of Benedictine life, and this massive dedication of time to prayer is one of the most obvious elements that distinguish monasticism from the life of the city.

There is perhaps scope for concern regarding the status of Eucharistic celebration. Here we have to note that there has been a development in doctrine and devotion since the time of Benedict, whose Eucharistic practice was considerably less than what is now commonly expected. Today we seem to be moving away from the excesses of the recent past, but it may be queried whether we are not in danger of marginalizing sacramental practice. In many male communities there has been a healthy reaction against clericalism that has led to significant changes in the style of celebration and also to a lower proportion of monks being presented for priestly ordination. In female communities it is becoming increasingly difficult to find suitable chaplains. Given that priestly ordination is excluded, the desire among women for greater leadership of their own worship understandably leads to an increasing reliance on non-sacramental liturgies.

As if nothing had changed, most official documents continue to emphasize the centrality of the Eucharist.

> No community can be built if it does not have its roots and core in the celebration of the most holy Eucharist, from which should spring as a consequence, all formation in community spirit.[117]

How this works out in practice is another question. It seems to me that there is a declining confidence in the whole sacramental reality—whether it be Eucharist, reconciliation, or anointing of the sick. It is not always a matter of explicit doctrine, simply a question of reduced interest. In part this may be due to a greater appreciation of the apophatic aspects of spirituality, and the fact that moving towards a Zen-like neutralism removes us from the spheres of theological controversy and community politics. On the other hand Neo-Pelagianism, which reduces everything to will-power and effort, may have a role to play. Once grace is taken out of the equation, the rituals that are seen to impart grace become irrelevant.

Another example of the impoverishment resulting from such reductionist tendencies can be seen in the rituals of monastic profession and consecration. It is a shame to reduce solemn profession to a ceremony that accompanies the making of vows. Active consecration and passive consecration are inseparable. The blessing of a monk or nun is an act of the Church that, according to long-standing monastic tradition, has baptismal-like effects in the life of the newly professed.[118]

3. A Lifestyle Worthy of the Gospel

Throughout this book we have been returning to the notion that the specificity of the Benedictine vocation needs to be expressed by a distinctive philosophy and lifestyle, each supporting the other. Beliefs and values are not much use unless and until they are embodied in practice. Practice, be it ever so holy, can become self-defeating unless the values it represents are internalized and appropriated.

We have seen that fidelity to many Benedictine values is at odds with many of the priorities we have acquired in the course of growing up. Typical among the substitutions that we are expected to weather in the process of growing into monastic life are the following:

- stability instead of mobility;
- humility instead of ambition, status-seeking, and pride;
- patience instead of anger, recrimination, and revenge;
- obedience instead of autonomy;
- common order instead of spontaneity;
- working without remuneration instead of being paid;
- discipline instead of relaxation;
- poverty instead of affluence;
- chastity instead of sexual liberation;
- celibacy instead of family life;
- silence instead of communication;
- abstemiousness in food and drink instead of satisfaction;

- early rising instead of sleeping late;
- early to bed instead of partying.

Show that list to any of our contemporaries and they will conclude that you lead a miserable life. And so you will—unless there is something else. It is this "something else" that makes monastic life tolerable, worthwhile, and sometimes delightful. Among the benefits we receive from belonging to a monastic community are the following:

- our relationship with God in prayer;
- our discipleship of Christ;
- the gift of daylong liturgy;
- our belonging to a sound spiritual tradition;
- our clarity about goals and means;
- the support and affection of like-minded brothers or sisters;
- our contemplative ambiance;
- our hours of holy leisure;
- our opportunities for spiritual, intellectual, and personal formation and growth;
- our relative freedom from financial and other worries.

Yet all these blessings lose their savor if they are not integrated within the search for God and the commitment to gospel values, as embodied in our particular way of life. Monasticism is a package: Some of its features are desirable, but they are inseparable from necessary renunciations. These are not impositions that we rightfully resent, but part of what we have freely chosen. Jesus prefaced his demand for absolute poverty with the conditional phrase, "If you **wish** to be perfect" (Mt. 19:21). The choice is ours: After fully manifesting the hard and difficult passages to be encountered on the journey towards God, Benedict solemnly reminds the aspirant: "This is the rule under which you

wish to serve; if you can observe it, enter; but if not, freely leave" (58:10). Selective observance is unacceptable. We are expected to commit ourselves to the whole.

No doubt there will always be discussion concerning the boundaries between essential monastic observances and little local rituals or antique carry-overs. We have to be cautious, however, in distinguishing too dramatically between what is substantive and what is symbolic. In the sacramental universe, of which the monastery is a part, the symbolic is often more than a decoration or an optional extra. In a way analogous to the sacraments, the ritual or symbol contains, conveys, and strengthens the reality it signifies.

Let us reflect on a single example from the Rule. Serving in the refectory is more than an equitable means of food distribution. Read Benedict's chapter; he says mutual service increases love (35:2). The week's serving is begun and ended with common prayer, and its high point is a ritual re-enactment of Christ's washing the disciples' feet at the Last Supper (35:9). This is more than a practical chore. If I excuse myself because I am too important or unwilling to serve, I will almost certainly cut myself off from something precious. Benedict realizes that such service is sometimes taxing and always inconvenient, but prefers to give additional help rather than disqualify someone from this means of grace. The way in which this service is rendered will differ from how it was done in Benedict's day and, perhaps, how it was done forty years ago. The important thing is not antiquarian fidelity, but the recognition of the values involved and the willingness to express them practically in whatever way works best. If we eliminate the symbol there is a danger that we are simultaneously weakening the reality.

If you were to read through the whole Rule, noting those passages that prescribe some kind of symbolic action, you will be surprised at how many there are. It is quite a good project to do this and to link the practices with their under-lying beliefs and values, and then to see how they fit into

Benedict's system as a whole. Distinctive modes of monastic behavior are signs of a different worldview; without some material expression, it is hard to see the values surviving.

One of the most distinctive monastic symbols is the habit. What we wear proclaims what we are. It may be that we have a more complex identity than heretofore, and, as a result, we wear different clothes in the liturgy, in community, and "outside"—whether this involves professional activity or recreation. Insisting that one size fits all is probably the best way to politicize the monastic habit, to polarize opinion, and to cause resentment. There is need for a lot of common sense. My own community has a story about a former Abbot General, who had been a cavalry officer, demonstrating, with the aid of two chairs, how to ride a horse in the habit. Once he was out of the house, his suggestion was cheerfully abandoned for reasons of safety, practicality, and hygiene, but it left in its wake a feeling of frustration at not being understood. The question of the monastic habit is especially delicate among Benedictine women.[119] The emotions aroused are an indication of the importance of the values that fuel the discussion. For those who can accept it, however, the wearing of distinctive vesture can be a badge of identity that strengthens a sense of belonging, a sign of poverty and renunciation, and a reminder to ourselves first and maybe to others, of the holiness of the life we have freely embraced.

Monastic distinctiveness is a quality that should be present in the mind as well as in behavior. It does not seem unreasonable to assume that years of living in vital contact with the Mystery would leave an imprint on the mind and heart of monks and nuns, so that when they study theology, or teach or write about it, a different character is detectable. Just as the experiential theology of twelfth-century Cistercian authors has been seen to inhabit a different universe from that evident in emergent Scholasticism, so it is to be hoped that even today monastic theologians will emerge who will embrace and propagate a theology that reflects their years of daily exposure to Scripture liturgy and the holy community. This is a theology that has much appeal today because it has substance; it is not "emotionally hollow, esthetically meaningless and spiritually empty."[120] But, for the most part, it is yet to be created.

Inevitably very few have the grace or moral strength to live gospel values in their entirety, and, as we have already said, such universal perfection would rob the community of its opportunities for tolerance and endurance. When deviations from the ideal become the rule rather than the exception the result is disedification, which is especially harmful during the formative years. Then, and at other crucial periods, when present hardship has to be weighed against future hopes, there needs to be some means of leapfrogging ambient negativity and bad example.

One simple means of doing this is by seeking alternative models in the lives of the great monastic figures of monastic history—to be inspired by their purer example to continue striving for the realization of the ideals we share with them. We all know that, in the past, there have been problems with hagiography when the authors were so keen to edify that they ended up by turning the saints into angels. This may have been a splendid victory for divine grace, but it is not particularly encouraging for those of us whose attitudes and actions are far from angelic. There is a serious need for good biographies of great monks and nuns, saints and near-saints who can serve as models for us in troubled times. We know that hagiographical and anecdotal literature was a great favorite of medieval monks, delivering the same message as loftier tomes, but in a more accessible manner. A picture is worth a thousand words—Benedict himself recognizes that those too dense to profit from wise words may yet be instructed by good example.

William of Saint-Thierry, a friend of Bernard and a Benedictine abbot who became a Cistercian, understood the important role played by the saints in helping us to avoid the pitfalls of too much abstraction. In the saints the working of grace is concrete and visible. By looking at their lives, identifying with them to some extent, we can see what possibilities there are for us if God's work is not hampered. Like many of the other early Cistercians, William considered that genuine holiness was somaticized—it progressively became evident even in the physical appearance of the saints. In this way it was able to have an influence of the lives of others. Of such saints he wrote the following:

> They do not form pictures of your love in their own likeness, but your love, finding in them simple matter, forms them and conforms them to itself both in feeling and in action, so that— apart from the glory and riches that are interior and hidden in the house of good conscience— the interior light shines forth in their outer countenance, not by some artful contrivance, but naturally. The attractive simplicity of their face and bearing provokes love of you even in boorish and uncivilized souls. The mere sight [of the saints] leads to compunction and love of you. In [the saints] nature returns to its origin.[121]

The transformation of the saints is not merely for their own benefit—they are intended to be sources of light and encouragement for us, even at several degrees of separation.

> Lord, you have made the darkness of our unknowing and our human blindness into a concealment of your face. Nevertheless around you is the light-filled tent of your saints who because of their association with your fire were themselves sources of light and heat, and by their word and example they have enlightened and inflamed others. To us they proclaim the solemn

joy of this most excellent knowledge [which will be ours] in the future life. By means of this knowledge we shall see you as you are, face to face. Meanwhile through the saints the lightning flashes of your truth light up the world and sparkle. Those with sound sight rejoice at this, but those who love darkness rather than light are disturbed and troubled.[122]

It would, of course, be desirable to live amid a cloud of holy witnesses, but too often familiarity breeds contempt. It takes a simple eye and a pure heart to perceive the holiness of the rough diamonds among whom we live. At the same time we have a need for models, especially in our early years. There is, therefore, a role for religious and monastic biography, or hagiography, though perhaps more critically written than in the past. Meeting the great figures of our tradition and learning from their writings can be a great source of inspiration and encouragement; sometimes we can get to the point of feeling a certain friendship with them and a reliance on their intercession for us as we still struggle on the same road that led them, by God's grace, to glory.

13 | *Perseverance*

If he promises perseverance
in his stability
RB 58:9

To begin a good work is, undoubtedly a noble endeavor, but it is worth nothing unless we allow the grace of God to bring to completion what it has initiated. This is true in any avocation and in every spiritual journey. In a Benedictine or Cistercian monastery, however, perseverance takes a specific form because it means actively continuing and concentrating on the same basic task year after year, decade after decade. The fact that we seem to be living longer and the world is changing more rapidly only intensifies the challenge involved in honoring our commitment to be faithful to the monastic life until death.

It would be wrong, however, to emphasize only the dogged character of monastic stability. Life in a monastery has its delightful moments. These are almost always the fruit of monastic discipline; a pure heart is able to find much joy in prayer, in fraternal communion, in the beauty of nature, and in the uplift from culture. These are not pleasures that detract from the integrity of daily adherence to an ordered way of life, nor are they merely moments of grim relief eked out of the unyielding granite of a miserable existence. They are necessary components of monastic experience: Without joy God is absent.

1. Sacred Space

In entering a monastery one does more than change residence, subscribe to a particular code of behavior, or achieve membership in a particular group. A monastery is a living reality. What is asked of newcomers is that they enter into the life of the community. They cannot continue to be what they were, lightly modified to adapt to a different setting. They have to begin to become something else. Something else, not someone else. For the process of transformation to be set in motion there must be some loosening of the grip of previous conditioning. Although teaching, personal direction, and good example are essential elements of monastic formation, it is even more important that a novice is able to absorb the atmosphere, to feel spiritually at home in the new ambiance. Entering a monastery is a spiritual homecoming.

> Let him be glad that he has, at last, found a dwelling place where he can live, not unwillingly, but voluntarily, for the rest of his life. Let him drive away every care about moving and let him make up his mind so that, being at peace, he can give himself only to the careful following of the exercises of a holy and well-tried way of life.[123]

Unless newcomers learn to feel relaxed in the monastery they will never become permeated by its spirit. They will be reduced to moral striving: rigidly obeying perceived rules, conforming to perceived best practice, and trying to ignore the feelings of alienation that this excess of effort yields. In the long run such vigilant busyness is self-defeating. It does not result in the naturalness that Benedict regards as the outcome of genuine good habit (7:68). A monastic vocation cannot be forced. Will-power is not enough. There needs to be some pre-existing affinity that guarantees that growth in monasticity is also growth in authentic selfhood.

This connaturality means that often a candidate is attracted to a particular monastery without quite knowing why. It may be the scenic location, the sense of silence and calm, the quiet industry, the disciplined freedom, the generalized aura or contentment, the sound of the chant, or the understanding smile of a member of the community. Some trivial aspect of daily life awakes a deep inner resonance within that signals to inquirers that this is not only a place where they can seek and serve God, it is also the possibility for them to be and become themselves.

To regard the monastery as sacred space requires a fair amount of subtlety of mind. There are many practical tasks to be done, differences to be endured, conflicts to be resolved. It is too easy to become caught up in the challenge of daily living so that one fails to see the mystery in which one is immersed. Reducing monastic life to a sequence of more or less holy works to be performed, robs it of its charm and its capacity to sustain and nourish a vocation. This is God's house, *domus Dei*—Benedict usurps the phrase used in the Vulgate to describe the theophany to Jacob (Gen. 28:17). This is where it is possible for us to encounter God—even to struggle with God. This is more than a dwelling of bricks and mortar.[124] Our approach to this place must be spiced with reverence. I am reminded of a verse in Elizabeth Barrett Browning's poem *Aurora Leigh*:

> Earth's crammed with heaven
> and every common bush afire with God.
> But only he who sees takes off his shoes,
> the rest sit around and pick blackberries.

It is true that the blackberries must be picked, but it is important that they do not become the major pre-occupation in a monastery. There are deeper mysteries into which, if we consent, we will be drawn.

Visitors occasionally remark on the sacredness that pervades a monastery, how it evokes in them a spiritual awareness that is normally latent. In the different ambiance conversions occur, not because of anything that was said or heard, but simply because in stepping outside their familiar world, they are confronted with a different side of themselves. Like travelers in a foreign country they find themselves responding to events in a way that would surprise those who know them at home. For many today, especially those who are unchurched or impatient with institutionalized religion, a monastery can become their spiritual home.

It is a pity that we who live in this sacred space become habituated. Permit me to exaggerate a little. We tend to lose our sense of wonder and try to make it more "normal." Boundaries are breached so that the *claustrum* becomes open to those who pay no heed to its sanctity. Material austerity that points beyond itself to the world of spiritual reality is sacrificed to comfort and modernity. Aimless chatter permeates its hallowed precincts. Even the church can become a place of tourism and singing practice, so that the oratory is no longer what its name signifies (52:1). The end result is that the place itself no longer calls us to recollection and prayer; instead it becomes an accomplice in our dissipation.

A supportive environment is a powerful help to perseverance. Any who have lived for a time in less-than-ideal surroundings will tell you what a relief it is to return to normal monasticity, how much easier it is to flow with the current than to struggle against it. There is much challenge to be met in a lifelong fidelity to the ordinary practices enjoined by the Rule. Sometimes we will feel disinclined to invest much effort in them. It is in such periods that we can be carried along by sound communal practice and a prevailing climate of monasticity.

Sacredness depends not on topography or architecture but on quality of life which, in turn, takes its character from those who live there. There is a need for some structures to preserve the distinctiveness that flows from generations of monastic living. Whatever the idiocies associated with the interpretation of canonical enclosure in the past, it needs to be recognized that too many foreign invasions undermine the monastic seriousness of the community. Hospitality is fine if it means welcoming visitors into our space; if it involves habitual compromise of monasticity then we are the losers, and our visitors stand to gain nothing. Similar observations hold with regard to external activities. Discernment needs to ascertain whether they truly contribute to the monastic project or whether they subvert it or serve merely as some compensatory mechanism. We remember that Benedict made provision to reduce the need for monks to leave the monastic space "because this is not at all good for their souls" (66:7). Despite many contrary historical precedents, a monk outside his monastery is like a fish out of water—long-term survival may indicate that he has evolved into a different species.

2. Not Giving Up

Mobility is one of the prime features of modern life. People move around more, not only geographically but also in terms of their work, relationships, and commitments. Coupled with this is the sense of life as a vast supermarket, in which we are confronted with a range of products among which we have the right to choose. The fact that the products are identical apart from their packaging and are often made by the same manufacturers does not bother us. We want the freedom to choose; we have the security of knowing that if we become dissatisfied with something there are alternatives available. The same hedging of bets occurs in seeking employment, in entering marriage, or entering religious life. We like to know that there is a backup in case things go wrong. We like to be able to cut our losses, as the saying goes.

We are most reluctant to burn our bridges. We see examples of this in pre-nuptial contracts where the partners make provision against their eventual breakup. We see it also in religious who are reluctant to dispossess themselves fully before solemn vows, in case things do not work out. It is important to realize that the taking of precautions against failure often makes it easier to fail. Knowing that there is a safety net can make us negligent in doing whatever we have to do to avoid falling. As the number of divorces and annulments increases, there is plenty of statistical evidence to support opting out. We issue press releases justifying our decision with acceptable psychobabble. Others pretend to believe it, fearful lest they might have to use it themselves someday.

In such a social climate the idea of committing ourselves to perseverance seems imprudent, if not lunatic. Everything changes so rapidly that we do not know what tomorrow will bring. This is where it is important to emphasize that the vow of stability is not based on the non-variability of community life, the Church, or society. Stability is grounded on the unchanging fidelity of God. It may be true that it was all so different before everything changed, and that in the course of a lifetime many major adaptations are demanded. It is our faith in God's fidelity that enables us to weather whatever storms come our way. Another image of stability is a building designed to withstand earthquakes. Contrary to our untutored expectations, the building is designed to sway with the movements of the earth rather than to stand solidly unmoving throughout the tremors. If it moves it survives; if it attempts to resist the movement it cracks open.

Stability comes from the verb *stare*, to stand. We all know that it is very difficult to remain standing for a long period without moving. The best way to remain upright is not to stay still but to keep walking. We can walk for much longer periods than we can stand, because the various muscle systems are alternately worked and rested. Stability is not immobility. It is the knack of remaining constant in the midst of change. The best example of this is a surfer. He knows that to get up and stay up on his surfboard he needs to be aware of the movement of wind and water so that he can subtly adjust his centre of gravity. The best way to persevere is to keep growing. This will not occur without periods or relative slackness and occasional wobbles, but the important thing is to keep moving forward, to keep adapting to changed circumstances and to re-orient oneself towards the goal. As St. Bernard implies, it is stability that prevents us from coming to grief when circumstances are adverse. "The contract of stability rules out henceforth any feeble relapse, angry departure, aimless or curious wandering and every vagary of fickleness."[125]

Stability is not a commitment to sameness. On the contrary it is a springboard that projects us into the future and ensures that the charism does not atrophy. As such it is an ongoing call to transcendence, not an excuse for nesting in the present. This is how Sister Helen Lombard explained this paradox:

> To live within our history, individually and together, as a *cenobium*, rooted in Christ, with a listening ear, a discerning heart, open to continuing conversion, free to hear the call of the Spirit in our *today*, and daring and courageous enough as Benedictine women to respond to go *beyond*.

> This is ultimately the challenge and the amazing
> paradox of stability.[126]

The magic of stability lies in a sustained and dynamic application of the means that lead most surely to the goal we have chosen. Often this means taking a long-term view of life. We are all prone to suffer from what has been termed the "instant gratification syndrome": We feel that something is wrong unless the desired outcome quickly follows on the initiation of the process. The trick in monastic life, as in so many other projects, is to see the linkage between short-term chores and long-term aims. This is not always an easy task, since in some cases the laws of cause and effect do not apply in monasteries. Union with God, innocence of life, progress in prayer, and affective community do not always succumb to Promethean striving. More often they result from the contrary experience of failure and neediness. This means that often we have to keep plodding on, even when everything seems to indicate that our effort is vain.

It is precisely this peasant-like plodding that is at risk in our slick, results-oriented culture. Benedict thinks that the monk, as he progresses to the top, goes through a stage of seeing himself as little more than a beast of burden (7:50). Certainly he is to be denied the glory of achieving perfection, but equally certain is the truth that he will never be beyond the pale of God's mercy. Opting out of the achievement race is one of the ways in which the monk distinguishes himself from his contemporaries. He knows that his relatives and friends hope that he will be a "success" as a monk, and perhaps that is also his unconscious ambition. Ultimately, however, it is in the promises of God that he places his hope. Such unrewarded fidelity is not very glamorous to behold or exciting to endure, but it indicates a solid attachment to God that all the drama of achievement can scarcely rival.

There is very little mystery about perseverance—it simply involves making use of the means that monastic life offers, day by day and year by year, and having confidence in God. Perseverance is not a matter of gritting one's teeth in difficult times or stretching oneself forward to cross the finishing line. As Benedict notes, it begins on Day One (58:9). It is a matter of really committing oneself (as distinct from "making a commitment") to give one's best to the monastic process and to stay with it while it works its magic on us. Grace is working on us to neutralize the natural fecklessness of the will; what we have to do is to avoid interfering with the process.

A good community provides us with a style of life that renders perseverance more plausible: the standard monastic observances, good spiritual directors, quality affective relationships, generativity, creative work, transparent and participatory governance, feedback, realistic boundaries, balanced days and seasons, appropriate relaxations. The list could be extended. The point to notice, however, is that perseverance is as much a quality of the community as it is of the individuals who are its members. To the extent that such qualities as those listed above are lacking, a community loses its adhesive grip and individuals more easily fall away. These apostasies will often be ascribed to subjective causes, and sometimes this is accurate. In many cases, however, the affective climate of the community and its governance have been contributory factors, perhaps allowing discontent to fester untended for fear of disturbing the status quo or, at the other extreme, steamrolling changes that many neither need nor want.

Stability is neither progressive nor conservative. Its strength lies in its attention to the present moment, like the peasant at his plow, concentrating on the job at hand and not much looking up from it. Yet the labor is sustained by the hope of a harvest. It is not for nothing that he works. Salvation is a matter of hope; for the moment stability helps to ensure that the furrows run true.[127]

3. Reaping the Benefits

Stability of place is not meant to protect us from earthquakes. Nor is it meant to provide a safe haven for agoraphobics. The restrictions of geographical mobility and the sober sameness of the living environment have another purpose. Stability of place and its contingent expressions such as enclosure are traditional means of securing stability of mind—*stabilitas mentis*. This enduring equanimity was recognized by the monastic tradition as a usual precondition for contemplative prayer. Years of heartfelt monastic observance produce a certain monasticity of thought and imagination—a conversion of memory that complements the more outward conversion of manners. It is part of the effect of low-impact living that we have the opportunity to undergo a purification of our mental faculties.

We know how memories can persist without our being fully in control of them, sometimes forming larger clusters with correspondingly greater clout. Childhood experiences of petty injustice can link up with recent events to produce a generalized mistrust of those with power over us. Humiliations continue to rankle years after they happen, causing us to blush with shame or become angry. The touches and inner warmth and excitement of a deep relationship linger to increase the bathos of loneliness. Dormant anger can be rekindled by a thought and surge unchecked until we are overwhelmed by rage. Pornographic images can continue to stimulate even after a different lifestyle has been embraced. Even when outward behavior is well-ordered, thoughts, affections, imaginations, and feelings still easily run riot.

The potential tyranny of obsessive or seasonally obsessive thoughts was well known to monastic tradition, as the writings of Evagrius and John Cassian attest. Who among us has not become suddenly conscious of wistful thoughts of home, family, friends, freedom, culture, holidays, hobbies, work, career, achievement? They drift in from nowhere and whiteout whatever contentment we have built up over the years, making us unnecessarily miserable and, often, ready to blame others for our joyless existence.

The prescription we find in the ancient writers is that we become vigilant and proactive concerning our thoughts and imagination. Sometimes this involves submitting them to conscious scrutiny in order to discover what they are trying to tell us. Often, however, it is a matter of intervening decisively to stop escaping from the present by half-living in the past or daydreaming about a possible future. Living mindfully involves limiting all forms of escapism, not only those that are frivolous, but more so the serious concerns that sometimes hijack our attention and concern. To achieve a good level of serious interior recollection we need to exercise some control over the sense-impressions and images that cross our paths. Constantly seeking to be entertained by the pursuit of novelties of one kind or another is a most effective way of blocking any progress toward contemplation. *Carpe diem!* We need to seize the opportunity that the present offers and to live it to the full.

The sustainability of our commitment demands that we are proactive in ordering our life. In particular it means nipping in the bud any tendency to lead a double life by blurring the boundaries between good and evil, so that large areas are accepted as morally neutral. We cannot afford to be vague. Behavior inconsistent with the commitments we have made usually begins at the level of thought. Long before any overt infidelity a mental betrayal has occurred that is not reversible without great self-honesty and considerable effort. This is why Benedict follows the tradition in recommending exposure of our thoughts to a spiritual senior (Prol. 28, 4:50). Our divided heart is the source of these conflicting thoughts; unless we are alert we can find ourselves drawn willy-nilly in opposite directions.

By bringing them into awareness we can confront them directly and, supported by the senior's presence, make a choice.

The effect of vigilance coupled with the sharing of thoughts is simplicity of life and lightness of spirit. Whether we recognize it or not, the presence of contrary imaginations blunts both our mental acuity and our feeling-response to everyday events. Giving a clear direction to our actions in line with our goal reduces the dispersion of energies and induces a sober sense of well-being. The simple life is not a happy accident, nor does it result from the inability to envisage alternatives. Simplicity is a quality of a heart that is undivided; it is brought about by a long sequence of courageous decisions taken and implemented. Simplicity is not the elimination of complexity but the habit of making consistent choices within complexity. A simple lifestyle is one with an uncontested finality: It knows its ultimate and immediate goals, and provides access to the means by which these aims are realized. One who has freely chosen to adopt such a lifestyle finds the fullest freedom by making use of the means that lead most effectively to the goal. The essential monastic observances are not alien impositions to be resisted with adolescent truculence or revolutionary fervor, but they are well-trodden paths to the fulfillment of the monastic dream. Walking them avoids wasting time and energy. Persevering on these sometimes hard and rough roads (58:8) will finally lead to God.

It cannot be emphasized too much that stability is not drudgery; progressively it becomes a source of deep happiness. We observe the transitions that Benedict notes at the end of the chapter on humility. Effort becomes habit or second nature, which then becomes delight. Alternatively, fear is transformed into love (7:67–69). Far from dragging ourselves along in dread-filled compliance, "we *run* along the road of God's commandments with swelling heart and a sweetness of love that is beyond description" (Prol. 49). Following the guidance of the gospel according to Benedict's Rule is not merely a lifestyle, it is a way of life, a way that leads to more abundant life.

When Malcolm Muggeridge was making a TV documentary about the Cistercian monks in Scotland he elicited from one of the senior monks a reply that delighted him. In response to his question about monastic austerity the reply came, "It's a hard bed to lie on, but a soft bed to die on." The truth contained in this bit of doggerel is profound. Monastic life is demanding, but its exigencies make sense in the context of eternal life. And lest we become disheartened, sometimes we receive from God an anticipation of what awaits us. And along the way there are many collateral benefits.

The sacrifices involved in monastic life are frequently chronicled, but we ought not to forget the hundredfold. There is a certain beauty that is a consequence of spending most of one's life in a single pursuit, attached to one place, and living with the same people. We are at liberty to be ourselves, no longer hiding behind facades or masks. Yet this self is more than the fleeting persona of this present moment; it is a self that stretches expansively over many years and decades, full of seeming contradictions and subject to so many vicissitudes. We are surrounded by so many memories of times past, of people now in heaven, of projects completed or left undone, of trees planted, of griefs and joys. As we pass through the monastery and listen to the echoes embedded in its walls, the refrain we hear is, "This is your life." Because of these voices we are compelled to live at a high level of truthfulness, since we cannot escape from what we have been and still are. A strong sense of continuity develops, and a deeper feeling of acceptance. This is where I belong. This is my home. Here I live; here I will die. This has been the journey that God has called me to make, and throughout the various reversals of fortune God has never abandoned me. Here have I become a stranger to this earthly city only because I have become a citizen of the cloistral paradise. "This is truly an awesome place, the house of God, the gate of heaven" (Gen. 28:17).

Notes

Abbreviations

CChrM	Corpus Christanorum Continuatio Mediaevalis (Turnhout: Brepols)
CFS	Cistercian Fathers Series (Kalamazoo: Cistercian Publications)
CSQ	Cistercian Studies Quarterly
CSS	Cistercian Studies Series (Kalamazoo: Cistercian Publications)
PL	Patrologia Latina (Paris: Migne)
SBOp	Sancti Bernardi Opera (Rome: Editiones Cistercienses)
SChr	Sources Chrétiennes (Paris: Cerf)

Notes

1   Non-conformity with this age is primarily a matter of beliefs and values. It is not an advocacy of antiquarianism or neo-primitivism. It does not close off the possibility of dialogue with the age in which we live. On the contrary, it welcomes the opportunity for any fusion of horizons. It is not necessarily opposed to the search for relevance that is sometimes covered by the term "chronological inculturation"; nor is it so entrenched in the customs of a previous generation that it is resistant to *aggiornamento*. Non-conformity to this age is something to be sought in so far as it is a deliberate and common sense commitment to the distinctive beliefs and values that alone make monastic life meaningful.

2   Viktor Dammertz, "St. Benedict: Master of Religious Life," *Consecrated Life* 6.2 (1982), p. 251.

3   David Parry, *Households of God: The Rule of St. Benedict with Explanations for Monks and Lay People Today* (London: Darton, Longman & Todd, 1980), p. 12.

4   Twelfth-century Cistercians seemed to take it for granted that detachment from this age was essential for the realization of the monastic project. Isaac of Stella equates the desire for God that is the source of devotion with distaste for everything to do with the world: *Sermons 37:14*; SChr 207, p. 292. And Aelred of Rievaulx was convinced that one could love fully neither God nor neighbor so long as worldly loves prevailed: *Nemo enim perfecte diligit, qui aliquid in hoc saeculo concupiscit, Sermo* 8:12; CChrM 2a, p. 67.

5   Aelred chronicles a common problem: Novices often find that their previous spiritual fervor disappears after entry. *Mirror of Charity* II, Chapter 17.

6   "Two thirds of religious conversions are gradual, the result of intellectual and emotional quest. Only a third are sudden. Conversions usually occur to adolescents, the sudden ones early in one's teens, the slower ones later." Gary Wills, "God in the Hands of Angry Sinners," *New York Review of Books,* April 8, 2004; pp. 68–74.

7   "Self-promotion" is Terrence Kardong's rendering of *exaltatio.* "Here the meaning is moral and psychological: the persons are vaunting themselves and not waiting humbly for God's action." *Benedict's Rule: A Translation and Commentary* (Collegeville: Liturgical Press, 1996), p. 136.

8   "It's revealing of our psychotherapeutic view of humanity and of our blame-based culture that we are so persuaded that the quality and quantity of what we ingest is primarily reactive, that our eating habits are less a matter of will and agency than one of displaced response to an injury or harm we have suffered, more often than not in the distant past." Francine Prose, *Gluttony* (New York: Oxford University Press, 2003), p. 61.

9   Aelred of Rievaulx, *Sermons* 34:3; CChrM 2a, p. 279. Later in the same sermon Aelred speaks about some of the higher

reaches of spiritual experience, but warns, "What I want to communicate to you is that you do not come to this point by doing nothing or by taking it easy, but by labors, vigils, tears, and contrition of heart." *Sermons* 34:29, p. 285-86.

10   This is the conclusion of a paper given by Kallistos Ware, "The Way of the Ascetics: Negative or Affirmative" in Vincent L. Wimbush e.a. [ed.], *Asceticism* (New York: Oxford University Press, 1998), p. 13. The quotation is from Fr. Alexander Elchaninov.

11   Thus Isaac of Stella: Sermons 5:24; SChr 130, p. 160: "I ask you brothers, for what reason do you labor amid sweat, do you live in poor conditions, do you remain vigilant both in bodily exercises and in spiritual pursuits, so that once vices are eliminated and a pattern of good living is established, the virtues may be introduced so that you may, as good workers, 'live soberly, justly and piously in this world'?" His answer to the question is the same as Cassian's. Austerity contributes to the purity of heart in which the vision of God is possible.

12   John Paul II, *Reconciliatio et Paenitentia*, # 18.

13   Thomas Merton, "Inner Experience," CSQ 18 (1983), p. 3.

14   See William C. Bushell, "Psychophysiological and Comparative Analysis of Ascetico-Meditational Discipline: Toward a New Theory of Asceticism," in *Asceticism*, p. 560.

15   Speaking especially of Evagrius, Bernard McGinn writes: "A more complete investigation than can be given here would reveal that *apatheia* and *agape* can be considered as two sides of the same *katastasis* (state of soul), the goal of all ascetic effort and the necessary precondition for the pure prayer, the two stages of which lead to the 'essential *gnosis* of the Trinity.'" "Asceticism and Mysticism in Late Antiquity and the Early Middle Ages," in *Asceticism*, p. 67.

16   Thomas Merton, *The Climate of Monastic Prayer* (CSS 1; Spencer: Cistercian Publications, 1970), p. 121.

17   See Jean Leclercq, *Otia Monastica: Études sur le vocabulaire de la contemplation au moyen âge* (Rome: Herder, 1963).

18   Josef Pieper, *Leisure the Basis of Culture* (New York: Pantheon Books, 1952), p. 52.

19   Max Picard, *The World of Silence* (Wichita, KS: Eighth Day Press, 2002), pp. 18-19.

20   *Conferences* 9:6; SChr 54, pp. 45-46.

21   Don De Lillo, quoted in David Remnick, "Exile on Main Street: Don De Lillo's undisclosed underworld," *The New Yorker*, September 15, 1997, pp. 43 and 47.

22   S. Giora Shoham, *Society and the Absurd* (Oxford: Blackwell, 1974). See also M. Casey, art. "Acedia," in Michael Downey [ed.], *The New Dictionary of Catholic Spirituality* (Collegeville: Michael Glazier, 1993), pp. 4-5.

23   Bernard of Clairvaux, Sent 3:31; SBOp 6b, 85, 3-4.

24   Michael Crichton, *Timeline* (London: Arrow Books, 2000), pp. 442-443.

25   Michael Hanby, "The Culture of Death, the Ontology of Boredom, and the Resistance of Joy," *Communio* (Summer 2004), pp. 184-85.

26   This is one of the serious criticisms leveled at contemporary culture by Pope John Paul II in his encyclical *Veritatis splendor*.

27   Robert Hughes, "Why Watch It, Anyway?" *The New York Review of Books*, February 16, 1995, p. 38.

28   Thomas Merton, "Inner Experience: Problems of the Contemplative Life (VII)," CSQ 19.4 (1984), pp. 269-70.

29   This is highlighted by the title of Jean Leclercq's study of medieval monastic culture, *The Love of Learning and the Desire for God* (London: SPCK, 2nd ed., 1978).

30   Seneca, *De tranquillitate animae*, 9.

31   Athanasius of Alexandria, *Letter to Marcellinus*, 12.

32 Allan Bloom, "The Study of Texts," in *Giants and Dwarfs: Essays 1960–1990* (New York: Simon and Schuster, 1990), pp. 306-7.

33 Steven D. Driver, *John Cassian and the Reading of Egyptian Monastic Culture* (New York: Routledge, 2002), p. 109.

34 M. Casey, *Sacred Reading: The Ancient Art of Lectio Divina* (Liguori: Triumph Books, 1996).

35 Aelred of Rievaulx, *Sermones de Oneribus*, 2; PL 195, 364b.

36 Columba Stewart, *Cassian the Monk* (New York: Oxford University Press, 1998), p. 84.

37 Aelred of Rievaulx, *Sermones de Oneribus* 27; PL 195, 473d-474a.

38 Aelred of Rievaulx, *Sermones* 19:10; CChrM 2a, p. 149.

39 Note the word "unnecessary." Some disasters have very positive effects, often because they make it impossible for us to continue to hide from the truth. Even though a crisis may destroy the precarious harmony we seemed to have achieved, we may find, as we pick up the pieces and put them back together, that something positive has been gained in the process.

40 Gregory the Great, *Moralia* 21:31 (CChr 143a, pp. 1065-66. Speaking of the need for restraint of the senses he writes, "Whoever unguardedly looks out through these windows of the body will often fall unwillingly into sinful delight."

41 Aelred of Rievaulx, *Sermones* 19:20; CChrM 2a, p. 151.

42 Aelred of Rievaulx, *Sermones* 3:18: CChrM 2a, p. 31.

43 A. W. Richard Sipe, *Celibacy: A Way of Loving, Living, and Serving* (Alexandria, NSW: E. J. Dwyer, 1996), p. 53.

44 Isaac of Stella, *Sermons* 31:14; SChr 207, p. 190.

45 See M. Casey, "*Suspensa Expectatio*: Guerric of Igny on Waiting for God," in *Studies in Spirituality* 9 (1999), pp. 78–92.

46   Augustine of Hippo, *On Psalm 29* 2.1; CChr 38, p. 174.

47   Richard Sipe, *A Secret World: Sexuality and the Search for Celibacy* (New York: Brunner-Routledge, 1990), p. 239.

48   Sipe, *Celibacy*, p. 54.

49   *Mirror for Novices*, 11; in Stephen of Sawley, *Treatises* (Kalamazoo: Cistercian Publications, 1984), p. 103.

50   Bernard of Clairvaux, Adv 4:5; SBOp 4:185, 9-7.

51   *Exordium Cistercii*, 1.

52   Such a situation was parodied by Bernard of Clairvaux in his *Apologia* 23. Needless to say, he is using irony, exaggerating the situation to make a point. "To distinguish between invalids and those who are well, the sick are bidden to carry a walking-stick in their hands. This is an obvious necessity, for the sick has to support the pretense of illness where there is no sign of pallor or emaciation. Should we laugh or cry at such foolishness? Is this the way Macarius lived? Is it Basil's teaching or Antony's command? Did the Fathers in Egypt adopt such a manner of life?" Trans. M. Casey in *Bernard of Clairvaux: Treatises I* (Spencer: Cistercian Publications, 1970), pp. 58-59.

53   PP 2:2; SBOp 5:192,19. See M. Casey, "The Meaning of Poverty for Bernard of Clairvaux," *Cistercian Studies Quarterly* 33.4 (1998), pp. 427–438.

54   *Exordium Parvum*, 16.

55   Bernard of Clairvaux, *Apologia*, 28; p. 65.

56   See M. Casey, *A Guide to Living in the Truth: Saint Benedict's Teaching on Humility* (Liguori: Triumph Books, 2001).

57   Aelred of Rievaulx, *De Oneribus* 12; PL 195, 407d.

58   See Guerric of Igny, *Advent Sermons* 3:1; SChr 166, p. 118. "It is most certain that our last day will come to us, but it is most uncertain when or where or how it will come except, as has been said, 'For the old death waits at the door, for the young it lies in ambush.'" The same theme, perhaps derived

from Cicero's *De Senectute* 20:74, is found in Bernard's *Sermon on Conversion*, 16.

59   In some rituals the one being professed lies prostrate on the floor during the prayers of monastic consecration, covered with a funeral pall. Of course there is a resurrection afterwards.

60   An ancient alternative of this is found in Juvenal's *Satires* (10:22): *Cantabit vacuus coram latrones viator.* "The empty-handed traveler will sing before robbers." One who has nothing has nothing to lose.

61   For the "obedience which is faith" see Romans 1:5 and its inclusive parallel at Romans 16:26. On obedience as an abiding disposition see also Romans 15:18, 16:19; 2 Corinthians 7:15, 10:5; 1 Peter 1:2.

62   Dorotheos of Gaza, *Instruction 5* #68, SChr 92, p. 264.

63   See T. G. Kardong, "Self-will in Benedict's Rule," *Studia Monastica* 42.2 (2000), pp. 319–46.

64   RB 5:7–10, like the chapter on humility, is description rather than prescription. This point is well made by Charles Dumont, "The Mystery of Obedience According to Saint Benedict and Saint Gregory," *Tjurunga* 23 (1982), pp. 5–19; 24 (1983), pp. 4–10; 25 (1983), pp. 36–41.

65   This is the scenario that Bernard of Clairvaux dramatizes in his third parable: *The Story of the King's Son Sitting on His Horse.* Translated by M. Casey in *Bernard of Clairvaux: The Parables & The Sentences* (CFS 55) (Kalamazoo: Cistercian Publications, 2000), pp. 45–49.

66   Guerric of Igny, *Sermons* 14:7, SChr 166, p. 302.

67   Bernard of Clairvaux, *Sermons of Psalm 90* 2:1-2, SBOp 4, pp. 389-390.

68   Aelred of Rievaulx, *Sermones*, 38:17-18; CChrM 2a; p. 310.

69   Aelred of Rievaulx, *De Oneribus* 13; PL 1995, 411b.

70   Augustine of Hippo, *On Psalm 99* 12; CChr 39, p. 1401.

71 Bernard of Clairvaux, *Sententiae* 1:26; SBOp 6b, 16, 13–17: "There should be two walls in a community; one inner and one outer. The inner wall is composed of those who are enclosed (*claustrales*), the outer wall of officials (*oboedientiales*). . . . There is rarely peace between these."

72 Sr. Helen Lombard SGS, "Mutual Obedience: An Aborted Effort?—Chapter 71," *Tjurunga* 53 (1997), p. 74. Many of Helen's ideas will be found in this chapter.

73 See M. Casey, "Merton's Teaching on the 'Common Will' and What the Journals Tell Us," *The Merton Annual* 12 (1999), pp. 62–84.

74 See M. Casey, *Fully Human, Fully Divine: An Interactive Christology* (Liguori: Triumph Books, 2004), pp. 35–42.

75 Here, apart from my own impressions, I am relying on Simon Baron-Cohen, *The Essential Difference: The Truth about the Male and Female Brain* (New York, Basic Books, 2003). The thesis of the book is stated succinctly on the first page: "The female brain is predominantly hard-wired for empathy. The male brain is predominantly hard-wired for understanding and building systems." The author is professor of psychology and psychiatry at Cambridge University.

76 Baldwin of Forde, *Spiritual Tractates* 15; trans. David N. Bell (CFS 41; Kalamazoo: Cistercian Publications, 1986), pp. 183–185.

77 Adalbert de Vogüé, *Community and Abbot in the Rule of Saint Benedict: Volume Two* (CSS 5/2) (Kalamazoo: Cistercian Publications, 1988), p. 430.

78 "Most often an intense mentor relationship ends with strong conflict and bad feelings on both sides." Daniel J. Levinson e.a., *The Seasons of a Man's Life* (New York: Ballantyne Books, 1978), p. 100.

79 Bernardo Olivera, "Our Young—and not so Young—Monks and Nuns: Aspects of our Monastic Formation from an Anthropological Point of View," conference given at the OCSO General Chapters, September 2002.

80   Ep 73, 2; SBOP 7, 180, 1–5, 14-15.

81   See M. Casey, "Adding Depth to our Response to Local Culture," in Peter Malone [ed.], *Discovering an Australian Theology* (Homebush: St. Paul Publications, 1988), pp. 121–30.

82   Of course sometimes self-expression cuts loose from its service of the common good, for example, if an organist were to assail the ears of worshipers with atonal bombast, or a cook were to replace familiar stodge with exotic portions of *cuisine nouvelle*. Both the music and the food may be high-class and bring great satisfaction to their creators, but such labors will not strengthen communal bonds unless the end- users can connect with what is being offered them. For their part, other members of community will probably resist any effort to reduce their habitual level of Philistinism if they do not clearly perceive that the initiators are acting from the heart of the community and not importing something foreign from "outside."

83   John Paul II, Letter to Cardinal Casaroli, *L'Osservatore Romano* (Weekly Edition in English), June 28, 1982, p. 7.

84   John Paul II, *Address to UNESCO* on June 2, 1980, #7; *L'Osservatore Romano*, June 23, 1980, p. 9. In this and the quotations that follow I have made some slight changes with a view to rendering the language more inclusive.

85   *Address to UNESCO*, #12; p. 10.

86   John Paul II, *Address to Eminent Personalities of the Brazilian Cultural World*, Rio de Janeiro, July 1, 1980, #1; *L'Osservatore Romano* July 14, 1980, pp. 3-4.

87   William of Saint-Thierry, *First Life of Saint Bernard I*, VII, 35; PL 185, 247-48.

88   *Descriptio positionis seu situationis monasterii Clarae-Vallensis*, PL 185; 571-72. A translation of the full text can be found in Pauline Matarasso, *The Cistercian World: Monastic Writings of the Twelfth Century* (Harmondsworth: Penguin, 1993), pp. 287–92.

89   Bernard of Clairvaux, *Miscellaneous Sermons* 42,4; SBOp
        6a, p. 258, lines 16–23.

90   Utopia (a good place) is in fact Atopia (no place), as is
        indicated by Samuel Butler's title *Erewhon*, an anagram for
        "nowhere." Some Utopias, such as B. F. Skinner's *Walden
        Two,* seem to me decidedly unpleasant places. It has been
        noted that, in the latter half of the twentieth century, many
        authors were more comfortable writing about Dystopia
        (a bad place). Think of George Orwell's *1984* or Aldous
        Huxley's *Brave New World* and films such as *Mad Max* and
        the like. The switch in emphasis possibly indicates a move-
        ment away from anthropological optimism in the direction
        of existential despair.

91   Quoted in *The Bulletin,* July 28, 1987, p. 27. The founder
        felt that, without an external point of reference, Moora
        Moora had become "more a reflection of a society than an
        alternative to it."

92   This section draws on the relevant parts of a previous article.
        M. Casey, "Desire and Desires in Western Tradition," in
        Desire: To Have or Not to Have (Canberra: The Humanita
        Foundation, Occasional papers 2, 2000), pp. 3–31.

93   Thomas J. Csordas, *The Sacred Self: A Cultural
        Phenomenology of Charismatic Healing* (Berkeley:
        University of California Press, 1994), pp. 157-58.

94   On this, see M. Casey, *Fully Human, Fully Divine: An
        Interactive Christology* (Liguori: Triumph Books, 2004).

95   *In Numeros homilia* 10, 2; PG 12, col 639a. Quoted in
        M. Casey, "The Virtue of Patience in Western Monastic
        Tradition," in *The Undivided Heart: The Western Monastic
        Approach to Contemplation* (Petersham: St. Bede's
        Publications, 1994), pp. 96–120.

96   See E. E. Malone, *The Monk and the Martyr: The Monk
        as the Successor of the Martyr* (Washington: Catholic
        University of America Press, 1950).

97   In Timothy Fry and others. [ed.], *RB 1980: The Rule of St. Benedict in Latin and English with Notes* (Collegeville: Liturgical Press, 1981), p. 361.

98   This distinction is important for the understanding of Thomas Merton's teaching on contemplative practice. See M. Casey, "Merton's Notes on 'Inner Experience': Twenty Years Afterwards," in *The Undivided Heart,* pp. 189–217, especially pp. 195–201.

99   See M. Casey, "Desire as Dialectic" in *Athirst for God,* especially pp. 251–80 (The Theme of Alternation).

100   John of Forde: *Sermons on the Song of Songs* 24 5: CChrM 17, p. 205: "Whoever you are, O soul, that aspire to the delights of love, do not recoil from its bitternesses if you wish to taste its sweetnesses. . . . You have submitted to an excessively delicate yoke of love if you are content only with its joys and will not have anything to do with the tiresome and disagreeable things that are part of the business of love and necessarily present themselves to those who walk in its ways."

101   Aelred of Rievaulx, *De Oneribus* 25; PL 195, 463d.

102   "Penitence at the state of the former person brings to birth a new person with pain and groaning. When this new person has a relapse and returns to the former life, which happens often. . . ." Augustine, *In Ps. 8,* 10 (CChr 38, p. 54).

103   QH 2.1-2; SBOp 4.390.8–23. See SC 17.2; SBOp 1.99.14–21. See also M. Casey, *Fully Human, Fully Divine,* pp. 106–112.

104   See M. Casey, "In Pursuit of Ecstasy: Reflections of Bernard of Clairvaux's *De Diligendo Deo,*" *Monastic Studies* 16 (1985), pp. 139–56.

105   See M. Casey, *Fully Human, Fully Divine,* pp. 3–10.

106   "The Spirituality of the Church of the Future," in *Theological Investigations: Volume XX: Concern for the Church,* translated by Edward Quinn (London: Darton, Longman

& Todd, 1981), pp. 148-149. On this see M. Casey, *Fully Human, Fully Divine*, pp. 201–19.

107   This was the issue addressed in my article "Mystical Experiences: The Cistercian Tradition," *Tjurunga* 52 (1997), pp. 64–87. See also Aquinata Böckmann, "Benedictine Mysticism: Dynamic Spirituality in the Rule of Benedict,' *Tjurunga* 57 (1999), pp. 85–101.

108   John Cassian, *Conferences* 9:8; SChr 54, pp. 48-49.

109   John Cassian, *Conferences* 9:26; SChr 54, p. 63.

110   Bernard of Clairvaux, *Sermon for St. John the Baptist*, 1; SBOp 5, 176, 17–22. See also *Sententiae* 1:18; SBOp 6b, 13, 1-2: "The temple of God is holy, and you are the temple of God. The temple of God is the religious house."

111   Bernard of Clairvaux, *Sermons for the Ascension* 6:13; SBOp 5, 158, 3–6. The subject of the first sentence is "Truth," but it is clear that it refers to Christ. Bernard also does not like corners, which he regards as the breeding-ground of individualism (*singularitas*); in a reference that may reflect the state of men's monasteries rather than women's he notes, "Where there is a corner there is probably dirt and mildew": *On the Lovableness of God* 34; SBOp 3, 149,8.

112   Aelred of Rievaulx, *Sermones*, 1:33-34; CChrM 21, pp. 10-11.

113   Bernard of Clairvaux, *Sermons for Septuagesima* 2:3; SBOp 4, 352, 2–14. I have deleted two phrases that refer to the text of Genesis 15:9-10 on which Bernard was commenting, but which, in the present context, have the effect of obscuring the flow of thought.

114   "The most significant fact about the time in which we are living is that it is a time in which a single movement of secularization is bringing peoples of all continents into its sweep." Thus Leslie Newbigin, *Honest Religion for Secular Man* (London: S.C.M. Press, 1966), p. 11. Some of the books from this period seem frightfully outdated today, yet once they caused a great stir. John A. T. Robinson, *Honest*

to God (London: S.C.M. Press, 1963). John A. T. Robinson and David L. Edwards, *The Honest to God Debate* (London: S.C.M, 1963). Paul van Buren, *The Secular Meaning of the Gospel* (London: S.C.M, 1963). Harvey Cox, *The Secular City* (New York: Macmillan, 1965). Daniel Callahan [ed.], *The Secular City Debate* (New York: Macmillan, 1966). Harvey Cox, *The Feast of Fools: A Theological Essay on Festivity and Fantasy* (Cambridge Mass: Harvard University Press, 1969). E. L. Mascall, *The Secularisation of Christianity* (London: Darton, Longman & Todd, 1965). Robert L. Richard, *Secularisation Theology* (London: Burns & Oates, 1967). Thomas J. J. Altizer, *The Gospel of Christian Atheism* (Philadelphia: Westminster Press, 1966). Thomas J. J. Altizer, *Toward a New Christianity: Readings in the Death of God Theology* (Harcourt, Brace & World, 1967). John Macquarrie, *God and Secularity* (Philadelphia: Westminster Press, 1967).

115   Speaking about the changed expectations and hopes expressed by a new generation of younger church-goers, Andrew Hamilton, S.J., writes: "Individual confession, visits to Churches and rituals that encourage a sense of transcendence will retain a place, particularly for young adults who discover them afresh. . . ." "Forty Years Away," *Eureka Street* 12.8 (October 2002), p. 37.

116   This can be noticed both in styles of music and in ritual action; in the latter proclamation may be replaced by conversation, and solemnity may be abandoned in favor of casual slouching. Among the many channels of influence affecting the liturgy is the cinema. "[T]he way Catholic liturgy is portrayed on the large or small screen directly shapes people's expectations of it." Richard Leonard, "Celluloid Celebrations," *Liturgy News* 30.2 (June 2000), p. 3.

117   *Presbyterorum ordinis*, 6.

118   See M. Casey, "Sacramentality and Monastic Consecration," *Word and Spirit* 18 (1998), pp. 27–48.

119   For a discussion of this see Kathleen Norris, *The Cloister Walk* (New York: Riverhead Books, 1996), pp. 317–28.

120   The phrase is lifted from Robert M. Pirsig, *Zen and the Art of Motorcycle Maintenance: An Inquiry into Values* (London: Corgi Books, 1976), p. 110. See M. Casey, "Emotionally Hollow, Esthetically Meaningless and Spiritually Empty: An Inquiry into Theological Discourse," *Colloquium* 14.1 (October 1981), pp. 54–61.

121   William of Saint-Thierry, *Meditative Prayers*, 12; PL 180, 247bc.

122   William of Saint-Thierry, *Meditative Prayers*, 7; PL 180, 228d-229a.

123   Anselm of Canterbury, *Letters* 1:21; PL 158, 1096-97

124   See Bernard of Clairvaux *Sermons for the Dedication of the Church* 6:1; SBOp 5, 396, 16-17: "Does God care about stones? It is not [the dedication' of walls but of people."

125   Bernard of Clairvaux, *Treatise on Precept and Dispensation* 44; SBOp 3, 284, 7-9.

126   Helen Lombard S.G.S., "The Profession of Stability: A Response," *Tjurunga* 58 (2000), p. 14.

127   On the notion of stability see M. Casey, "The Value of Stability," *Cistercian Studies Quarterly* 31.3 (1996), pp. 287–301.